NIST CLOUD SECURITY

CYBER THREATS, POLICIES, AND BEST PRACTICES

4 BOOKS IN 1

BOOK 1

NIST CLOUD SECURITY 101: A BEGINNER'S GUIDE TO SECURING CLOUD ENVIRONMENTS

BOOK 2

NAVIGATING NIST GUIDELINES: IMPLEMENTING CLOUD SECURITY BEST PRACTICES FOR INTERMEDIATE USERS

BOOK 3

ADVANCED CLOUD SECURITY STRATEGIES: EXPERT INSIGHTS INTO NIST COMPLIANCE AND BEYOND

BOOK 4

MASTERING NIST CLOUD SECURITY: CUTTING-EDGE TECHNIQUES AND CASE STUDIES FOR SECURITY PROFESSIONALS

ROB BOTWRIGHT

Published by Rob Botwright
Library of Congress Cataloging-in-Publication Data
ISBN 978-1-83938-677-0
Cover design by Rizzo

Disclaimer

The contents of this book are based on extensive research and the best available historical sources. However, the author and publisher make no claims, promises, or guarantees about the accuracy, completeness, or adequacy of the information contained herein. The information in this book is provided on an "as is" basis, and the author and publisher disclaim any and all liability for any errors, omissions, or inaccuracies in the information or for any actions taken in reliance on such information. The opinions and views expressed in this book are those of the author and do not necessarily reflect the official policy or position of any organization or individual mentioned in this book. Any reference to specific people, places, or events is intended only to provide historical context and is not intended to defame or malign any group, individual, or entity. The information in this book is intended for educational and entertainment purposes only. It is not intended to be a substitute for professional advice or judgment. Readers are encouraged to conduct their own research and to seek professional advice where appropriate. Every effort has been made to obtain necessary permissions and acknowledgments for all images and other copyrighted material used in this book. Any errors or omissions in this regard are unintentional, and the author and publisher will correct them in future editions.

BOOK 1 - NIST CLOUD SECURITY 101: A BEGINNER'S GUIDE TO SECURING CLOUD ENVIRONMENTS

BOOK 2 - NAVIGATING NIST GUIDELINES: IMPLEMENTING CLOUD SECURITY BEST PRACTICES FOR INTERMEDIATE USERS

BOOK 3 - ADVANCED CLOUD SECURITY STRATEGIES: EXPERT INSIGHTS INTO NIST COMPLIANCE AND BEYOND

BOOK 4 - MASTERING NIST CLOUD SECURITY: CUTTING-EDGE TECHNIQUES AND CASE STUDIES FOR SECURITY PROFESSIONALS

Introduction

Welcome to the NIST Cloud Security book bundle, a comprehensive guide to navigating the complexities of securing cloud environments in today's digital landscape. As organizations increasingly adopt cloud technologies to drive innovation and agility, the importance of robust security measures cannot be overstated. With cyber threats evolving at an alarming rate, it is imperative for security professionals to stay ahead of the curve and implement best practices that align with industry standards and regulatory requirements.

This book bundle comprises four essential volumes, each tailored to address the needs of different audiences, from beginners to seasoned security professionals. In "NIST Cloud Security 101: A Beginner's Guide to Securing Cloud Environments," readers will embark on a journey to understand the fundamental concepts and principles of cloud security. From the basics of cloud computing to key security considerations, this book provides a solid foundation for those new to the field.

Moving on to "Navigating NIST Guidelines: Implementing Cloud Security Best Practices for Intermediate Users," intermediate users will find practical insights into implementing NIST's best practices. This volume explores the intricacies of NIST guidelines and offers guidance on how to effectively implement security measures that align with these standards.

For those seeking to deepen their understanding of NIST compliance and explore advanced security strategies,

"Advanced Cloud Security Strategies: Expert Insights into NIST Compliance and Beyond" provides invaluable expertise. This book dives into advanced techniques, emerging threats, and expert insights to help readers enhance their security posture and stay ahead of evolving risks.

Finally, "Mastering NIST Cloud Security: Cutting-Edge Techniques and Case Studies for Security Professionals" equips seasoned security professionals with the tools and techniques needed to tackle complex challenges head-on. Through cutting-edge techniques, real-world case studies, and expert analysis, this volume empowers readers to master NIST compliance and safeguard their organizations against the most sophisticated cyber threats.

Together, these four books form a comprehensive guide to NIST cloud security, offering a holistic approach to securing cloud environments and mitigating cyber risks. Whether you're just beginning your journey into cloud security or looking to enhance your expertise, this book bundle is your go-to resource for understanding, implementing, and mastering NIST compliance in the cloud.

BOOK 1

NIST CLOUD SECURITY 101

A BEGINNER'S GUIDE TO SECURING CLOUD ENVIRONMENTS

ROB BOTWRIGHT

Chapter 1: Understanding Cloud Computing Basics

Cloud deployment models play a crucial role in shaping the infrastructure of modern businesses. Understanding these models is essential for organizations seeking to optimize their operations and maximize their resources in the cloud. One of the most common cloud deployment models is the public cloud, which offers resources and services to the general public over the internet. Public cloud providers such as Amazon Web Services (AWS), Microsoft Azure, and Google Cloud Platform (GCP) offer a wide range of services, including computing power, storage, and networking, on a pay-as-you-go basis. This model is highly scalable and flexible, making it ideal for startups and small businesses looking to minimize upfront costs and quickly scale their operations. Another popular deployment model is the private cloud, which is dedicated to a single organization and typically hosted either on-premises or by a third-party provider. Private clouds offer greater control and customization options compared to public clouds, making them suitable for organizations with specific security, compliance, or performance requirements. Hybrid cloud deployment models combine elements of both public and private clouds, allowing organizations to leverage the benefits of both environments. In a hybrid cloud setup, certain workloads or applications may run on-premises in a private cloud, while others are deployed in the public cloud. This flexibility enables organizations to optimize performance, security, and cost-effectiveness based on their unique needs. Multi-cloud deployment models involve using multiple cloud providers to host different aspects of an organization's infrastructure. This approach helps mitigate the risk of vendor lock-in and allows organizations to take advantage of best-of-breed services from different providers. However, managing multiple cloud environments can also introduce complexity and challenges in terms of interoperability, data management, and security. Choosing the right cloud deployment model depends on various factors, including the organization's goals, budget, technical requirements, and regulatory considerations. Before deciding on a deployment model, organizations should conduct a thorough assessment of their needs and evaluate the strengths and weaknesses of each option. Once a deployment model has been selected, organizations can begin the process of deploying their infrastructure in the cloud. This typically involves provisioning virtual machines, configuring networking and security settings, and deploying applications and services. Cloud providers offer a range of tools and services to streamline the deployment process, including Infrastructure as Code (IaC) tools like AWS CloudFormation and Azure Resource Manager, which allow organizations to define their infrastructure as code and automate the deployment process. Additionally, containerization technologies such as Docker and Kubernetes provide a lightweight and portable way to package and deploy applications across different cloud environments. By understanding the various cloud deployment models and leveraging the right tools and techniques, organizations can harness the power of the cloud to drive innovation, agility, and growth. Whether they opt for a public, private, hybrid, or multi-cloud approach, organizations stand to benefit from the scalability, flexibility, and cost-effectiveness of cloud computing. As the cloud continues to evolve and mature, businesses that embrace these deployment models will be better positioned to adapt to changing market dynamics and stay ahead of the competition. Cloud service models are fundamental to understanding how cloud computing works. At its core, cloud computing offers a range of services and resources over the internet, allowing users to access computing power, storage, and other resources on-demand. One of the most common cloud service models is Infrastructure as a Service (IaaS), which provides virtualized computing resources over the internet. With IaaS, users can provision and manage virtual machines, storage, and networking infrastructure without having to invest in physical hardware. Popular IaaS providers include Amazon Web Services (AWS), Microsoft Azure, and Google Cloud Platform (GCP). Another widely used cloud service model is Platform as a Service (PaaS), which provides a platform for developing, deploying, and managing applications over the internet. PaaS offerings typically include development tools, middleware, and runtime environments, allowing developers to focus on building and deploying applications without worrying about underlying infrastructure. Examples of PaaS providers include Heroku, Microsoft Azure App Service, and Google App Engine. Software as a Service (SaaS) is perhaps the most user-friendly cloud service model, offering ready-to-use software applications over the internet. With SaaS, users can access applications such as email, productivity suites, and customer relationship management (CRM) tools through a web browser or mobile app, eliminating the need for installation and maintenance. Common examples of SaaS applications include Microsoft Office 365, Salesforce, and Google Workspace. Beyond these primary cloud service models, there are also specialized offerings such as Function as a Service (FaaS) and Database as a Service (DBaaS). FaaS allows developers to deploy individual functions or pieces of code in response to events, paying only for the compute time consumed. AWS Lambda and Azure Functions are popular FaaS offerings. DBaaS, on the other hand, provides managed database services, allowing users to offload database administration tasks such as provisioning, scaling, and backup to the cloud provider. Examples of DBaaS offerings include Amazon RDS, Azure SQL Database, and Google Cloud SQL. Deploying cloud service models typically involves interacting with the cloud provider's management console or using command-line interface (CLI) tools. For example, to provision a virtual machine in AWS using the CLI, users can use the aws ec2 run-instances command, specifying parameters such as instance type, security groups, and key pairs. Similarly, deploying a web application to Azure App Service involves using the az webapp deploy command, along with parameters specifying the application package and target resource group. By leveraging cloud service models, organizations can access a wide range of computing resources and services on-demand, enabling greater agility, scalability, and cost-efficiency. Whether they're developing new applications, running mission-critical workloads, or simply collaborating with colleagues, cloud service models provide the foundation for modern digital transformation. As the cloud computing landscape continues to evolve, businesses that embrace these service models will be better positioned to innovate, compete, and thrive in a rapidly changing environment.

Chapter 2: Introduction to NIST Framework for Cloud Security

The NIST Framework for Improving Critical Infrastructure Cybersecurity, developed by the National Institute of Standards and Technology (NIST), is a comprehensive framework designed to help organizations manage and mitigate cybersecurity risks. At its core, the NIST Framework consists of several key components that provide a structured approach to cybersecurity risk management. The first component is the Core, which serves as the foundation of the framework and includes a set of cybersecurity activities and outcomes organized into five functions: Identify, Protect, Detect, Respond, and Recover. Each function is further broken down into categories and subcategories that outline specific cybersecurity activities and outcomes. For example, the Identify function focuses on understanding the organization's cybersecurity risk posture and includes categories such as Asset Management, Business Environment, Governance, Risk Assessment, and Risk Management Strategy. Within each category, organizations are encouraged to implement specific subcategories, such as creating an inventory of authorized and unauthorized devices for the Asset Management category. The second component of the NIST Framework is the Implementation Tiers, which provide a mechanism for organizations to assess and improve their cybersecurity risk management practices. There are four tiers: Partial, Risk Informed, Repeatable, and Adaptive, each representing a different level of cybersecurity risk management maturity. Organizations can use the Implementation Tiers to gauge their current cybersecurity capabilities and identify areas for improvement. The third component of the NIST Framework is the Framework Profile, which allows organizations to create a customized roadmap for improving their cybersecurity posture based on their specific needs and priorities. The Framework Profile is created by aligning the organization's cybersecurity activities and outcomes with the categories and subcategories outlined in the Core. This process helps organizations prioritize their cybersecurity investments and focus on areas where they have the greatest need or opportunity for improvement. Finally, the NIST Framework includes a set of informative references and additional guidance to help organizations implement the framework effectively. These resources include NIST Special Publications (SPs), industry best practices, and other cybersecurity frameworks and standards. By leveraging these resources, organizations can gain valuable insights and guidance on how to implement specific cybersecurity controls and practices. In summary, the NIST Framework for Improving Critical Infrastructure Cybersecurity is a flexible and scalable framework that provides organizations with a structured approach to managing and mitigating cybersecurity risks. By understanding and implementing the key components of the framework, organizations can strengthen their cybersecurity posture and better protect their critical assets and information from cyber threats. Mapping the NIST Framework to cloud security is essential for organizations seeking to align their cybersecurity efforts with industry best practices and standards. The NIST Framework, developed by the National Institute of Standards and Technology, provides a comprehensive set of guidelines and recommendations for improving critical infrastructure cybersecurity. When applying the NIST Framework to cloud environments, organizations must first understand the unique challenges and considerations associated with cloud computing. Cloud environments introduce complexities such as shared responsibility models, multi-tenancy, and dynamic resource provisioning, which can impact the implementation of cybersecurity controls. To effectively map the NIST Framework to cloud security, organizations should start by conducting a thorough assessment of their cloud infrastructure and identifying potential areas of risk. This assessment should include an evaluation of the organization's cloud service models (IaaS, PaaS, SaaS), deployment models (public, private, hybrid), and the specific cloud services and providers being used. Once the assessment is complete, organizations can begin mapping the NIST Framework's core components - Identify, Protect, Detect, Respond, and Recover - to their cloud security practices. For example, in the Identify function, organizations may need to identify and assess cloud assets, data, and applications to understand their cybersecurity risk posture. This could involve using cloud security tools and services to scan for vulnerabilities, assess data sensitivity, and classify assets based on their criticality. In the Protect function, organizations must implement appropriate security controls to safeguard their cloud environments against cyber threats. This may include configuring access controls, encryption, and network security measures to protect data and resources stored in the cloud. Organizations can leverage cloud-native security services provided by their cloud provider, such as AWS Identity and Access Management (IAM) and Azure Security Center, to implement these controls effectively. In the Detect function, organizations need to establish mechanisms for detecting and monitoring security incidents and anomalies in their cloud environments. This could involve deploying security monitoring tools, such as cloud-native logging and monitoring services, to collect and analyze telemetry data from cloud resources. By monitoring for unauthorized access attempts, unusual network traffic patterns, and other indicators of compromise, organizations can quickly identify and respond to potential security threats. In the Respond function, organizations must develop and implement incident response plans to address security incidents and breaches in their cloud environments. This may involve defining roles and responsibilities, establishing communication channels, and conducting regular incident response exercises to ensure readiness. Organizations can use cloud orchestration and automation tools, such as AWS CloudFormation and Azure Automation, to streamline incident response processes and facilitate rapid remediation of security incidents. Finally, in the

Recover function, organizations need to develop strategies for recovering from security incidents and restoring normal operations in their cloud environments. This may include implementing backup and disaster recovery solutions, testing restoration procedures, and conducting post-incident reviews to identify lessons learned and areas for improvement. By aligning their cloud security practices with the NIST Framework, organizations can enhance their cybersecurity posture and better protect their cloud assets and data from cyber threats. This involves integrating the principles and guidelines outlined in the NIST Framework into their cloud security policies, procedures, and technologies. Through continuous monitoring, evaluation, and improvement, organizations can ensure that their cloud environments remain secure, resilient, and compliant with industry standards and regulations.

Chapter 3: Risks and Challenges in Cloud Environments

Data privacy and confidentiality risks pose significant challenges to organizations in today's digital landscape. With the increasing volume of data being generated, collected, and processed, protecting sensitive information has become a top priority for businesses of all sizes and industries. Data privacy refers to the protection of personal and sensitive information from unauthorized access, use, or disclosure. Confidentiality, on the other hand, involves ensuring that only authorized individuals or entities have access to sensitive data. These risks can arise from various sources, including cyber attacks, insider threats, regulatory non-compliance, and third-party breaches. Cyber attacks such as data breaches, ransomware, and phishing attacks are among the most common threats to data privacy and confidentiality. Hackers and malicious actors target organizations' systems and networks to steal sensitive information, disrupt operations, or extort ransom payments. To mitigate these risks, organizations must implement robust cybersecurity measures, such as encryption, access controls, and threat detection systems, to safeguard their data from unauthorized access and tampering. Insider threats, including negligent or malicious employees, contractors, or partners, also pose significant risks to data privacy and confidentiality. These individuals may intentionally or unintentionally disclose sensitive information, misuse privileged access, or circumvent security controls, putting the organization's data at risk. To address insider threats, organizations should implement strict access controls, monitoring systems, and employee training programs to detect and prevent unauthorized activities and ensure compliance with security policies. Regulatory non-compliance is another key risk factor for data privacy and confidentiality. Organizations that fail to comply with data protection laws and regulations, such as the General Data Protection Regulation (GDPR) and the California Consumer Privacy Act (CCPA), may face severe penalties, fines, and reputational damage. To avoid these consequences, organizations must stay informed about relevant regulations, assess their data handling practices, and implement appropriate measures to ensure compliance. Third-party breaches, involving vendors, suppliers, or service providers, can also pose significant risks to data privacy and confidentiality. Organizations that share sensitive information with third parties must ensure that these entities have adequate security measures in place to protect the data. This may involve conducting due diligence assessments, establishing contractual agreements, and implementing monitoring mechanisms to ensure compliance with security requirements. Deploying robust data privacy and confidentiality measures requires a multi-faceted approach that addresses technical, operational, and regulatory aspects of cybersecurity. Organizations can leverage a variety of tools, technologies, and best practices to enhance their data protection capabilities. For example, encryption technologies, such as Secure Sockets Layer (SSL) and Transport Layer Security (TLS), can help encrypt data both in transit and at rest, preventing unauthorized access and tampering. Access control mechanisms, such as role-based access control (RBAC) and multi-factor authentication (MFA), can restrict access to sensitive information based on user roles and permissions, reducing the risk of unauthorized access. Data loss prevention (DLP) solutions can help organizations monitor, detect, and prevent the unauthorized transmission of sensitive data outside the organization's network, helping to mitigate the risk of data breaches and compliance violations. Additionally, organizations can implement employee training programs and security awareness initiatives to educate staff about the importance of data privacy and confidentiality and their role in safeguarding sensitive information. By adopting a proactive and holistic approach to data privacy and confidentiality, organizations can mitigate risks, protect their sensitive information, and maintain the trust and confidence of their customers, partners, and stakeholders.

Legal and compliance challenges are a critical consideration for organizations operating in today's complex regulatory environment. With the proliferation of data privacy and security regulations, such as the General Data Protection Regulation (GDPR), the California Consumer Privacy Act (CCPA), and the Health Insurance Portability and Accountability Act (HIPAA), organizations face increased scrutiny and accountability for how they handle sensitive information. These regulations impose strict requirements on organizations regarding data collection, processing, storage, and sharing, with significant penalties for non-compliance.

Organizations must navigate a complex web of legal requirements and regulatory obligations to ensure they meet their compliance obligations.

This involves understanding the scope and

implications of relevant regulations, assessing their applicability to the organization's operations, and implementing appropriate measures to achieve compliance. One of the key challenges organizations face is the complexity and ambiguity of regulatory requirements. Many regulations are written in broad terms, leaving room for interpretation and uncertainty about how they apply to specific situations. For example, GDPR's requirement for organizations to implement "appropriate technical and organizational measures" to protect personal data leaves room for interpretation, requiring organizations to exercise judgment and discretion in implementing security controls. Additionally, regulations often vary by jurisdiction, industry, and type of data, further complicating compliance efforts. Another challenge is the evolving nature of regulations, which are subject to change and revision over time. As new threats emerge and technologies evolve, regulators may update existing regulations or introduce new ones to address emerging risks and challenges. This dynamic regulatory landscape requires organizations to stay informed about regulatory developments, monitor changes to relevant laws and standards, and adjust their compliance strategies accordingly. Achieving compliance can also be resource-intensive and costly for organizations, particularly smaller businesses with limited resources and expertise. Compliance efforts may require significant investments in technology, personnel, and training to implement and maintain the necessary controls and processes. Additionally, organizations may need to engage legal counsel, consultants, or auditors to help navigate complex regulatory requirements and ensure compliance. Despite these challenges, non-compliance can have serious consequences for organizations, including fines, penalties, legal action, and reputational damage. Regulators have the authority to impose significant financial penalties for violations of data protection and privacy regulations, with fines potentially reaching millions of dollars or a percentage of annual revenue, whichever is higher. In addition to financial penalties, non-compliance can result in legal liability, lawsuits, and damage to the organization's reputation and brand. Moreover, organizations that fail to comply with regulatory requirements may lose the trust and confidence of customers, partners, and stakeholders, leading to loss of business and competitive disadvantage. To address legal and compliance challenges effectively, organizations must adopt a proactive and strategic approach to compliance management. This involves establishing a robust compliance program that encompasses policies, procedures, controls, and monitoring mechanisms to ensure compliance with applicable laws and regulations. Organizations should conduct regular risk assessments to identify potential compliance gaps and vulnerabilities and develop risk mitigation strategies to address them. Additionally, organizations should invest in ongoing training and education for employees to raise awareness about legal and compliance requirements and promote a culture of compliance throughout the organization. Leveraging technology and automation can also help streamline compliance efforts and reduce the burden on resources. For example, organizations can use compliance management software to centralize compliance activities, track regulatory changes, and automate compliance workflows. Similarly, organizations can deploy data governance and privacy management tools to help manage data lifecycle, enforce data retention policies, and ensure data protection and privacy compliance. By taking a proactive and holistic approach to legal and compliance challenges, organizations can mitigate risks, protect their interests, and maintain trust and confidence in the eyes of regulators, customers, and stakeholders.

Chapter 4: Fundamentals of Cloud Security Controls

Authentication mechanisms are fundamental to ensuring the security of digital systems and protecting sensitive information from unauthorized access. These mechanisms verify the identity of users and entities attempting to access a system or resource, helping to prevent unauthorized access and mitigate the risk of security breaches. There are various authentication methods and techniques used in modern computing environments, each offering different levels of security and usability. One of the most common authentication methods is password-based authentication, where users are required to provide a username and password to access a system or application. While passwords are widely used and familiar to users, they have several limitations, including susceptibility to brute-force attacks, password reuse, and weak password practices. To mitigate these risks, organizations should enforce strong password policies, such as requiring complex passwords, regular password changes, and multi-factor authentication (MFA) to add an extra layer of security. Multi-factor authentication (MFA) is an authentication method that requires users to provide two or more authentication factors to verify their identity. This typically involves combining something the user knows (such as a password) with something they have (such as a smartphone or security token) or something they are (such as a fingerprint or facial recognition). By requiring multiple factors for authentication, MFA significantly enhances security by reducing the risk of unauthorized access even if one factor is compromised. Organizations can deploy MFA using various methods, including SMS-based codes, mobile authentication apps, biometric authentication, and hardware tokens. Another authentication mechanism gaining popularity is biometric authentication, which uses unique biological characteristics such as fingerprints, facial features, or iris patterns to verify a user's identity. Biometric authentication offers a high level of security and convenience, as users do not need to remember passwords or carry physical tokens. However, biometric authentication systems may also present privacy and security concerns, such as the risk of biometric data theft or spoofing attacks. To mitigate these risks, organizations should implement robust security measures, such as encrypting biometric data, storing it securely, and implementing anti-spoofing mechanisms. In addition to traditional authentication methods, organizations can also leverage advanced authentication technologies such as federated identity management and single sign-on (SSO) to streamline authentication processes and improve user experience. Federated identity management allows users to access multiple applications and services using a single set of credentials, reducing the need for separate authentication mechanisms and simplifying user access management. Single sign-on (SSO) is a similar concept that enables users to authenticate once and access multiple applications and services without needing to re-enter their credentials. These technologies improve productivity, enhance security, and reduce the administrative burden associated with managing multiple user accounts and passwords. Deploying authentication mechanisms effectively requires careful planning, implementation, and ongoing management. Organizations should conduct a thorough risk assessment to identify authentication requirements, evaluate available authentication methods, and select appropriate solutions based on their security needs, user requirements, and regulatory compliance requirements. Once selected, organizations should implement authentication mechanisms following best practices and industry standards, such as NIST Special Publication 800-63 for digital identity guidelines. This may involve configuring authentication settings, integrating authentication mechanisms with existing systems and applications, and testing authentication processes to ensure they function as intended. Additionally, organizations should regularly monitor and review authentication logs, audit trails, and security events to detect and respond to suspicious activities or security incidents promptly. By implementing robust authentication mechanisms and following best practices, organizations can strengthen their security posture, protect sensitive information, and mitigate the risk of unauthorized access and security breaches. Encryption techniques play a crucial role in safeguarding sensitive information and ensuring the confidentiality and integrity of data in transit and at rest. Encryption is the process of converting plaintext data into ciphertext using cryptographic algorithms and keys, making it unreadable to unauthorized parties. There are various encryption techniques and algorithms available, each offering different levels of security and suitability for different use cases. One of the most widely used encryption techniques is symmetric encryption, where the same key is used for both encryption and decryption. Symmetric encryption algorithms, such as Advanced Encryption Standard (AES) and Data Encryption Standard (DES), are fast and efficient, making them suitable for encrypting large volumes of data. To encrypt data using symmetric encryption, users typically use a command-line interface (CLI) tool or programming library to specify the encryption algorithm, key, and plaintext data. For example, the OpenSSL command-line tool can be used to encrypt a file using AES encryption with the following command: openssl enc -aes-256-cbc -in plaintext.txt -out ciphertext.enc -k secretkey. This command specifies the AES-256-CBC encryption algorithm, reads plaintext data from the file plaintext.txt, encrypts it, and writes the ciphertext to the file ciphertext.enc using the secret key secretkey. Another encryption technique is asymmetric encryption, where a pair of keys - a public key and a private key - is used for encryption and decryption, respectively. Asymmetric encryption algorithms, such as RSA and Elliptic Curve Cryptography (ECC), offer stronger security guarantees and enable secure key exchange and digital signatures. To encrypt data using asymmetric encryption, the sender typically encrypts the data using the recipient's public key, which can be obtained from a public key infrastructure (PKI) or key exchange protocol. The recipient then decrypts the data using their private key. For example, the OpenSSL command-line tool can be used to encrypt a file using RSA encryption with the recipient's public key: openssl rsautl -encrypt -pubin -in plaintext.txt -out ciphertext.enc -inkey publickey.pem. This command reads plaintext data from the file plaintext.txt, encrypts it using the recipient's public key stored in the file publickey.pem, and writes the ciphertext to the file ciphertext.enc. In addition to symmetric and asymmetric encryption, there are also hybrid encryption techniques that combine the strengths of both approaches. Hybrid encryption involves using symmetric encryption to encrypt the data and then encrypting the symmetric key using asymmetric encryption. This approach provides the efficiency of symmetric encryption and the security of asymmetric encryption, making it suitable for a wide range of applications. To decrypt data encrypted using hybrid encryption, the recipient first decrypts the symmetric key using their private key and then uses the symmetric key to decrypt the data. Encryption techniques are essential for protecting sensitive information in various scenarios, including data storage, transmission over networks, and communication between devices. By understanding the principles of encryption and deploying appropriate encryption techniques, organizations can enhance the security of their data and minimize the risk of unauthorized access and data breaches. However, it's important to note that encryption is not a silver bullet and should be used in conjunction with other security measures, such as access controls, authentication mechanisms, and security monitoring, to provide comprehensive protection against cyber threats. Additionally, organizations should regularly update their encryption algorithms and keys, monitor for vulnerabilities, and adhere to industry best practices to ensure the effectiveness of their encryption strategies.

Chapter 5: Securing Data in the Cloud

Data classification and handling are fundamental aspects of data management and cybersecurity, essential for protecting sensitive information and ensuring compliance with regulatory requirements. Data classification involves categorizing data based on its sensitivity, importance, and potential impact on the organization, enabling organizations to apply appropriate security controls and protection measures. One common approach to data classification is to assign labels or tags to data based on its classification level, such as "public," "internal," "confidential," or "restricted." Organizations should develop a data classification policy that defines classification criteria, guidelines, and procedures for classifying data consistently and accurately. To classify data effectively, organizations should consider factors such as the data's value, sensitivity, legal and regulatory requirements, and potential impact on the organization if compromised. Once data has been classified, organizations must implement appropriate handling procedures to ensure that data is protected according to its classification level. This may involve encrypting sensitive data, restricting access to authorized personnel, and implementing secure storage and transmission mechanisms. Encryption is a widely used technique for protecting sensitive data, both in transit and at rest. Organizations can use encryption algorithms and keys to convert plaintext data into ciphertext, making it unreadable to unauthorized parties. To encrypt data using command-line interface (CLI) tools, organizations can use encryption utilities such as OpenSSL, which supports various encryption algorithms, including AES, RSA, and DES. For example, to encrypt a file using AES encryption with OpenSSL, organizations can use the following CLI command: openssl enc -aes-256-cbc -in plaintext.txt -out ciphertext.enc -k secretkey. This command specifies the AES-256-CBC encryption algorithm, reads plaintext data from the file plaintext.txt, encrypts it, and writes the ciphertext to the file ciphertext.enc using the secret key secretkey. Access controls are another critical aspect of data handling, ensuring that only authorized individuals or entities have access to sensitive information. Organizations can implement access control mechanisms, such as role-based access control (RBAC) and attribute-based access control (ABAC), to enforce access policies based on user roles, permissions, and attributes. RBAC assigns permissions to user roles, allowing organizations to manage access rights efficiently and securely. For example, organizations can use CLI commands to create user roles and assign permissions using cloud service providers' identity and access management (IAM) services, such as AWS IAM or Azure Active Directory. Additionally, organizations can use ABAC to define access policies based on attributes such as user attributes, resource attributes, and environmental attributes. Data handling procedures should also include guidelines for data storage, transmission, sharing, and disposal. Organizations should store sensitive data in secure locations, such as encrypted databases or file systems, and use secure transmission protocols, such as Transport Layer Security (TLS), to encrypt data in transit. When sharing data with third parties, organizations should use secure channels and implement data sharing agreements or contracts to ensure that data is handled securely and in compliance with applicable regulations. Finally, organizations must establish procedures for securely disposing of data when it is no longer needed. This may involve permanently deleting data from storage devices, securely erasing data from hard drives, or physically destroying storage media to prevent data leakage or unauthorized access. By implementing effective data classification and handling practices, organizations can mitigate the risk of data breaches, protect sensitive information, and maintain compliance with regulatory requirements. However, it's essential to regularly review and update data classification policies and handling procedures to adapt to changing business needs, technology advancements, and regulatory requirements. Additionally, organizations should provide training and awareness programs to educate employees about the importance of data classification and handling and their roles and responsibilities in safeguarding sensitive information. By fostering a culture of data security and accountability, organizations can minimize the risk of data loss, protect their reputation, and build trust with customers, partners, and stakeholders.

Data loss prevention (DLP) strategies are essential for organizations seeking to protect sensitive information and mitigate the risk of data breaches and leaks. DLP aims to prevent unauthorized access, use, or disclosure of sensitive data by monitoring, detecting, and blocking unauthorized activities in real-time. One of the key components of DLP strategies is data discovery, which involves identifying and classifying sensitive data across the organization's IT infrastructure. Organizations can use data discovery tools and techniques to scan systems, networks, and storage repositories for sensitive information, such as personally identifiable information (PII), financial data, intellectual property, and confidential documents. Command-line interface (CLI) tools such as PowerShell or Linux shell commands can be used to search for sensitive data in files and directories. For example, organizations can use PowerShell commands to search for credit card numbers in files stored on a Windows file server: Get-ChildItem -Recurse -File | Select-String -Pattern "\b\d{4}[-\s]?\d{4}[-\s]?\d{4}[-\s]?\d{4}\b". This command recursively searches for files in the specified directory and its subdirectories, then uses regular expressions to identify credit card numbers. Once sensitive data has been discovered and classified, organizations can implement controls and policies to prevent unauthorized access and transmission of sensitive information. This may involve encrypting data at rest and in transit, restricting access to authorized personnel, and implementing data loss prevention (DLP) solutions to monitor and enforce security policies. Encryption is a widely used technique for protecting sensitive data, ensuring that only authorized individuals or entities have access to the information. Organizations can use encryption algorithms and keys to convert plaintext data into ciphertext, making it unreadable to unauthorized parties. To encrypt data using command-line interface (CLI) tools, organizations can use encryption utilities such as OpenSSL, which supports various encryption algorithms, including AES, RSA, and DES. For example, to encrypt a file using AES encryption with OpenSSL, organizations can use the following CLI command: openssl enc -aes-256-cbc -in plaintext.txt -out ciphertext.enc -k secretkey. This command specifies the AES-256-CBC encryption algorithm, reads plaintext data from the file plaintext.txt, encrypts it, and writes the ciphertext to the file ciphertext.enc using the secret key secretkey. Access controls are another critical aspect of DLP strategies, ensuring that only authorized individuals or entities have access to sensitive information. Organizations can implement access control mechanisms, such as role-based access control (RBAC) and attribute-based access control (ABAC), to enforce access policies based on user roles, permissions, and attributes. RBAC assigns permissions to user roles, allowing organizations to manage access rights efficiently and securely. For example, organizations can use CLI commands to create user roles and assign permissions using cloud service providers' identity and access management (IAM) services, such as AWS IAM or Azure Active Directory. Additionally, organizations can use ABAC to define access policies based on attributes such as user attributes, resource attributes, and environmental attributes. Data loss prevention (DLP) solutions play a crucial role in detecting and preventing unauthorized access, use, or transmission of sensitive data. These solutions use a combination of technologies, including data discovery, content inspection, and policy enforcement, to monitor data flows and identify potential security incidents in real-time. When deploying DLP solutions, organizations should consider factors such as scalability, performance, integration with existing systems, and regulatory compliance requirements. Additionally, organizations should regularly review and update DLP policies and rules to adapt to changing threats and business needs. Employee training and awareness programs are also essential for the success of DLP strategies, ensuring that employees understand the importance of data security and their role in protecting sensitive information. By educating employees about security best practices, common threats, and the consequences of data breaches, organizations can reduce the risk of insider threats and human errors that could lead to data loss or leakage. Ultimately, effective data loss prevention (DLP) strategies require a combination of technology, policies, and employee awareness to protect sensitive information and safeguard the organization's reputation and trust.

Chapter 6: Identity and Access Management in Cloud Environments

Role-Based Access Control (RBAC) is a fundamental access control mechanism used in cybersecurity to manage user permissions and access rights within an organization's IT infrastructure. RBAC assigns permissions to users based on their roles and responsibilities within the organization, rather than individual identities or attributes. This approach simplifies access management by grouping users into roles based on their job functions, such as administrator, manager, or employee, and defining permissions associated with each role. CLI commands can be used to implement RBAC policies and manage user roles and permissions in various operating systems and applications. For example, in Linux systems, organizations can use the usermod command to add users to groups and assign group permissions. To add a user to a group in Linux, organizations can use the following CLI command: usermod -aG groupname username. This command adds the user specified by username to the group specified by groupname, granting them access to resources and permissions associated with that group. RBAC provides several benefits for organizations, including improved security, scalability, and ease of administration. By assigning permissions based on roles rather than individual users, RBAC helps organizations enforce the principle of least privilege, ensuring that users have access only to the resources and information necessary to perform their job functions. This reduces the risk of unauthorized access and data breaches, as users cannot access sensitive information or perform privileged actions without the appropriate permissions. Additionally, RBAC simplifies access management and administration by centralizing user permissions and reducing the number of access control lists (ACLs) that need to be managed. Instead of assigning permissions to individual users, administrators can assign permissions to roles, making it easier to manage access rights for large groups of users with similar job functions. RBAC also supports scalability, allowing organizations to easily add or remove users and adjust permissions as needed without having to modify individual user accounts or access control settings. This flexibility makes RBAC well-suited for dynamic and rapidly changing environments, such as cloud computing and software-as-a-service (SaaS) applications, where user roles and permissions may need to be adjusted frequently. To deploy RBAC effectively, organizations should follow best practices and principles for role design, implementation, and management. This includes conducting a thorough analysis of user roles and responsibilities, identifying common job functions and access requirements, and defining roles and permissions accordingly. Organizations should also establish procedures for granting and revoking role-based permissions, monitoring user activity, and auditing access rights to ensure compliance with security policies and regulatory requirements. RBAC can be implemented at various levels within an organization's IT infrastructure, including operating systems, databases, applications, and network devices. Many modern operating systems and applications provide built-in support for RBAC, allowing organizations to define roles and permissions using native tools and interfaces. For example, cloud service providers such as AWS, Azure, and Google Cloud Platform offer RBAC capabilities that allow organizations to define custom roles and assign granular permissions to users and groups. RBAC can also be implemented using specialized access control solutions and identity management platforms that provide advanced features such as role inheritance, role-based provisioning, and fine-grained access controls. These solutions help organizations enforce consistent access policies across heterogeneous IT environments and streamline access management processes. In summary, Role-Based Access Control (RBAC) is a powerful access control mechanism that helps organizations manage user permissions and access rights based on their roles and responsibilities. By assigning permissions to roles rather than individual users, RBAC improves security, scalability, and administration, making it an essential component of modern cybersecurity strategies. Single Sign-On (SSO) solutions are integral components of modern identity and access management (IAM) systems, streamlining authentication processes and enhancing user experience across multiple applications and services. SSO enables users to authenticate once and access multiple applications and services without the need to re-enter their credentials repeatedly. This significantly reduces the burden on users and simplifies access management for organizations. CLI commands can be used to configure and manage SSO solutions, particularly in cloud environments and identity providers that offer command-line interfaces for administration. For example, cloud service providers such as AWS and Azure provide CLI tools that allow administrators to configure SSO settings, manage user identities, and define access policies. To configure SSO in AWS using the AWS CLI, administrators can use the aws sso-admin command to create permission sets, associate users with permission sets, and manage SSO settings. SSO solutions typically rely on standard authentication protocols such as Security Assertion Markup Language (SAML) or OpenID Connect (OIDC) to facilitate single sign-on across different applications and services. SAML is a widely used XML-based protocol that enables secure authentication and authorization between identity providers (IdPs) and service providers (SPs). OIDC is a more modern and flexible authentication protocol based on the OAuth 2.0 framework, providing support for identity federation, user authentication, and single sign-on. To deploy SSO using SAML, organizations need to configure their identity provider (IdP) to authenticate users and generate SAML assertions, which are then sent to service providers (SPs) to grant access. This involves configuring trust relationships between the IdP and SPs, exchanging metadata, and defining access policies and attributes mappings. For example, in Okta, a popular identity provider, administrators can use the Okta Admin Console or the Okta CLI to configure SAML applications, define user attributes, and set up authentication policies. OIDC follows a similar authentication flow, where users authenticate with the IdP and obtain tokens, which are then used to access protected resources at SPs. OIDC provides support for features such as single sign-on, user authentication, token-based authorization, and identity federation, making it suitable for modern web and mobile applications. To deploy OIDC-based SSO, organizations need to configure their IdP and SPs to support OIDC, define client applications, scopes, and authorization policies, and implement token-based authentication and authorization mechanisms. This may involve using CLI commands or APIs provided by identity providers and application frameworks to configure OIDC clients, define authentication endpoints, and handle token validation and authorization. SSO solutions offer several benefits for organizations, including improved security, user experience, and administrative efficiency. By centralizing authentication and access control, SSO reduces the risk of password-related security incidents, such as phishing attacks, password reuse, and brute-force attacks. Users benefit from a seamless and consistent authentication experience, as they can access multiple applications and services with a single set of credentials. Administrators also benefit from simplified access management and reduced administrative overhead, as they can manage user identities, access policies, and security settings centrally. Additionally, SSO solutions support integration with identity and security management tools, such as multi-factor authentication (MFA), identity federation, and user provisioning, enhancing security and compliance capabilities. However, organizations should also consider potential challenges and limitations when deploying SSO solutions, such as compatibility issues with legacy applications, user adoption and training, and regulatory compliance requirements. By addressing these challenges and following best practices for SSO deployment, organizations can realize the full benefits of SSO, including improved security, user experience, and administrative efficiency.

Chapter 7: Network Security Considerations for Cloud Services

Virtual Private Clouds (VPCs) are a fundamental component of cloud computing environments, providing organizations with a private and isolated section of a cloud provider's infrastructure to deploy and manage their resources. CLI commands are often used to create and manage VPCs, allowing administrators to configure networking settings, security controls, and resource provisioning. For example, in Amazon Web Services (AWS), administrators can use the AWS Command Line Interface (CLI) or AWS Management Console to create VPCs, subnets, route tables, and security groups. VPCs offer several benefits for organizations, including improved security, network isolation, and flexibility in resource management.

By deploying resources within a VPC, organizations can create logical boundaries and enforce network segmentation, preventing unauthorized access and reducing the attack surface. Additionally, VPCs enable organizations to customize networking settings, such as IP address ranges, subnets, and routing policies, to meet their specific requirements and preferences. To create a VPC in AWS using the CLI, administrators can use the create-vpc command with the desired parameters, such as the CIDR block for the VPC and any optional settings. Once the VPC is created, administrators can configure additional networking settings, such as subnets, route tables, and internet gateways, to enable connectivity to the internet or other VPCs. Subnets are logical subdivisions of a VPC's IP address range, allowing organizations to segregate resources based on their networking requirements and access controls.

By creating multiple subnets within a VPC, organizations can isolate different types of resources, such as web servers, application servers, and databases, and apply specific security policies and routing rules to each subnet. To create subnets in AWS, administrators can use the create-subnet command with the desired VPC ID, CIDR block, and availability zone. Route tables are used to control the flow of network traffic within a VPC, specifying the destination for packets based on their IP addresses. Administrators can create route tables in AWS using the create-route-table command and associate them with subnets to define routing policies for traffic within the VPC. Security groups act as virtual firewalls for resources within a VPC, controlling inbound and outbound traffic based on user-defined rules. Administrators can create security groups in AWS using the create-security-group command and configure rules to allow or deny traffic based on criteria such as IP addresses, port numbers, and protocols. Internet gateways provide connectivity between a VPC and the internet, allowing resources within the VPC to communicate with external networks and services. To create an internet gateway in AWS, administrators can use the create-internet-gateway command and attach it to the VPC using the attach-internet-gateway command.

Once configured, administrators can use the AWS Management Console or CLI to manage and monitor VPC resources, including monitoring network traffic, configuring security settings, and scaling resources as needed. VPCs are a critical component of cloud infrastructure, providing organizations with the flexibility, scalability, and security required to deploy and manage their applications and services in the cloud. By leveraging VPCs effectively and following best practices for network design and security, organizations can build resilient and secure cloud environments that meet their business needs and regulatory requirements.

Network segmentation strategies are fundamental to modern cybersecurity, providing organizations with a powerful defense mechanism against cyber threats and unauthorized access. CLI commands are often used to implement network segmentation, allowing administrators to configure network devices, such as routers, switches, and firewalls, to enforce segmentation policies. For example, in a Cisco environment, administrators can use the Cisco IOS command-line interface to configure access control lists (ACLs), VLANs, and routing protocols to segment their networks effectively. Network segmentation involves dividing a network into smaller, isolated segments or zones based on criteria such as user roles, applications, data sensitivity, or security requirements. By creating separate network segments, organizations can contain the impact of security incidents, prevent lateral movement of attackers, and limit access to critical resources. To implement network segmentation, organizations should conduct a thorough assessment of their network architecture, identifying potential segmentation points, traffic patterns, and security requirements. This assessment helps organizations determine the most effective segmentation strategy and identify any existing vulnerabilities or misconfigurations that may impact security. Once the segmentation strategy is defined, administrators can begin implementing segmentation controls using CLI commands or network management tools.

One common approach to network segmentation is the use of virtual local area networks (VLANs), which partition a physical network into multiple logical networks, each with its own broadcast domain. VLANs enable organizations to isolate traffic and enforce security policies based on VLAN membership, helping to prevent unauthorized access and minimize the risk of network-based attacks. To create VLANs in a Cisco environment using the CLI, administrators can use commands such as vlan to create VLANs and interface to assign VLANs to specific network interfaces. Another approach to network segmentation is the use of access control lists (ACLs), which filter traffic based on predefined rules and criteria. ACLs can be applied to routers, switches, and firewalls to control traffic flows between network segments and enforce security policies, such as allowing or blocking specific protocols, IP addresses, or port numbers. To configure ACLs in a Cisco router using the CLI, administrators can use commands such as access-list to define ACL rules and interface to apply ACLs to specific interfaces. In addition to VLANs and ACLs, organizations can also implement segmentation at the application layer using firewalls, proxies, and other network security devices. These devices inspect and filter traffic based on application-layer protocols, such as HTTP, FTP, and DNS, allowing organizations to enforce fine-grained security policies and protect against application-level threats. To configure application-layer segmentation using firewalls, administrators can use CLI commands or management interfaces provided by firewall vendors to define rules and policies based on application characteristics and behaviors. Network segmentation is not a one-time task but an ongoing process that requires regular monitoring, maintenance, and updates to adapt to changing threats and business requirements. Administrators should regularly review segmentation policies, audit network configurations, and conduct penetration testing to identify and address any security gaps or vulnerabilities. Additionally, organizations should implement segmentation best practices, such as principle of least privilege, network zoning, and segmentation based on trust levels, to ensure effective security controls and minimize the risk of unauthorized access or data breaches. By implementing robust network segmentation strategies and following best practices for segmentation design and management, organizations can strengthen their cybersecurity posture, reduce the attack surface, and protect critical assets and data from cyber threats.

Chapter 8: Compliance and Regulatory Requirements in Cloud Computing

Industry-specific compliance standards play a crucial role in regulating and ensuring the security and integrity of data and operations within various sectors. These standards are developed by regulatory bodies or industry associations to address the unique challenges and requirements of specific industries, such as healthcare, finance, or education. CLI commands are often used to assess compliance with industry-specific standards, allowing organizations to automate compliance checks, generate audit reports, and remediate non-compliant configurations. For example, in the healthcare industry, organizations must comply with the Health Insurance Portability and Accountability Act (HIPAA), which sets standards for the protection of sensitive patient information and the secure transmission of electronic health records (EHRs). To assess compliance with HIPAA requirements using CLI commands, organizations can use tools such as AWS Config or Azure Policy to evaluate configurations, monitor changes to resources, and enforce compliance policies. Similarly, in the finance industry, organizations must adhere to regulations such as the Payment Card Industry Data Security Standard (PCI DSS), which governs the security of payment card data and transactions. CLI commands can be used to conduct PCI DSS compliance scans, identify vulnerabilities, and implement security controls to protect cardholder data. For example, organizations can use tools like Qualys or Nessus to perform vulnerability scans and penetration tests, identify security weaknesses, and remediate issues to comply with PCI DSS requirements. In the education sector, institutions must comply with regulations such as the Family Educational Rights and Privacy Act (FERPA), which safeguards the privacy of student records and prohibits the unauthorized disclosure of personally identifiable information (PII). CLI commands can be used to audit access controls, monitor data usage, and enforce data protection policies to ensure compliance with FERPA requirements. For example, organizations can use native auditing tools in cloud platforms or third-party solutions to track user activity, detect unauthorized access attempts, and maintain audit logs for compliance purposes. While industry-specific compliance standards vary in scope and requirements, they typically include common elements such as data protection, access controls, risk management, and incident response. Organizations must develop and implement comprehensive compliance programs that address these elements and align with industry standards and best practices. CLI commands can help organizations automate compliance tasks, streamline audit processes, and demonstrate adherence to regulatory requirements through documentation and reporting. However, achieving and maintaining compliance with industry-specific standards requires a collaborative effort involving IT teams, security professionals, compliance officers, and other stakeholders. Organizations must continuously assess their compliance posture, monitor changes to regulations, and update policies and procedures accordingly to address evolving threats and regulatory requirements. By investing in compliance initiatives and leveraging CLI tools and automation, organizations can strengthen their cybersecurity defenses, protect sensitive data, and build trust with customers, partners, and regulators in their respective industries.

Auditing and reporting in the cloud are essential processes for ensuring compliance, identifying security risks, and monitoring the health and performance of cloud environments. CLI commands are often used to automate auditing tasks, generate reports, and analyze cloud resources, allowing organizations to maintain visibility and control over their cloud infrastructure. For example, in Amazon Web Services (AWS), organizations can use the AWS Command Line Interface (CLI) to retrieve information about cloud resources, monitor resource usage, and analyze logs for security and compliance purposes. By leveraging CLI commands, organizations can streamline auditing processes and gain insights into their cloud environments. Auditing in the cloud involves reviewing configurations, access controls, and activities to ensure compliance with regulatory requirements and security best practices. Organizations must regularly audit their cloud environments to identify misconfigurations, unauthorized access, and potential security vulnerabilities. CLI commands can be used to audit various aspects of cloud environments, such as IAM policies, network configurations, and encryption settings. For example, organizations can use AWS CLI commands to list IAM users, roles, and policies, identify overly permissive permissions, and remediate issues to improve security posture. Reporting plays a crucial role in auditing and provides stakeholders with visibility into the state of cloud environments, compliance status, and security posture. CLI commands can be used to generate reports on resource utilization, access logs, compliance checks, and security incidents. For example, organizations can use AWS CLI commands to query CloudTrail logs, analyze CloudWatch metrics, and generate reports on user activity, API calls, and resource changes. By automating reporting tasks with CLI commands, organizations can streamline compliance audits, demonstrate adherence to security policies, and proactively identify and address security risks. Cloud service providers offer native tools and APIs that organizations can integrate with their existing systems to automate auditing and reporting processes. For example, AWS provides services such as AWS Config, AWS CloudTrail, and AWS CloudWatch, which enable organizations to monitor resource configurations, track user activity, and analyze performance metrics in real-time. Organizations can use AWS CLI commands to configure these services, retrieve data, and generate reports to support auditing and compliance efforts. Additionally, third-party security and compliance solutions offer advanced features for auditing and reporting in the cloud. These solutions integrate with cloud platforms, collect data from various sources, and provide centralized dashboards and reporting capabilities. Organizations can use CLI commands or APIs provided by these solutions to automate audits, analyze security events, and generate custom reports tailored to their specific requirements. Auditing and reporting in the cloud are continuous processes that require ongoing monitoring, analysis, and documentation. Organizations must establish policies, procedures, and controls to govern auditing activities, define metrics and thresholds for reporting, and ensure timely remediation of identified issues. By leveraging CLI commands and automation tools, organizations can enhance visibility, streamline auditing processes, and maintain compliance with regulatory requirements and security standards in their cloud environments.

Chapter 9: Incident Response and Disaster Recovery in the Cloud

Incident response planning is a critical component of cybersecurity strategy, enabling organizations to effectively detect, respond to, and recover from security incidents and data breaches. CLI commands are often used to automate incident response processes, coordinate actions among response teams, and execute remediation tasks to mitigate the impact of security incidents. For example, in the event of a security incident, organizations can use CLI commands to gather information about affected systems, analyze log files, and isolate compromised resources to prevent further damage. Incident response planning begins with the development of a comprehensive incident response plan (IRP) that outlines procedures, roles, and responsibilities for responding to security incidents. The IRP should define incident categories, severity levels, escalation procedures, and communication protocols to ensure a coordinated and effective response. CLI commands can be used to document the IRP, automate incident notification and escalation, and facilitate communication among incident response teams. For example, organizations can use CLI scripts to send notifications to designated contacts, trigger automated responses based on predefined criteria, and update incident status in real-time. The incident response plan should also include procedures for incident detection and classification, enabling organizations to quickly identify and assess the severity of security incidents. CLI commands can be used to configure monitoring tools, analyze log files, and detect anomalous behavior indicative of security threats. For example, organizations can use CLI commands to set up intrusion detection systems (IDS), configure log aggregation and analysis tools, and create custom alerts and notifications for suspicious activities.

Once an incident is detected and classified, organizations must initiate the response phase to contain the incident, minimize damage, and restore normal operations. CLI commands can be used to execute incident response procedures, such as isolating affected systems, disabling compromised accounts, and deploying security patches and updates. For example, organizations can use CLI commands to disable compromised user accounts, reset passwords, and revoke access permissions to prevent further unauthorized access. During the response phase, incident response teams must collaborate effectively to coordinate actions, share information, and make timely decisions to mitigate the impact of security incidents. CLI commands can be used to facilitate collaboration among response teams, such as sharing incident data, coordinating response activities, and documenting incident timelines and actions taken. For example, organizations can use CLI commands to create incident tickets, assign tasks to team members, and track progress toward incident resolution.

Following the containment and eradication of the incident, organizations must conduct a post-incident review to analyze the root causes of the incident, identify lessons learned, and implement improvements to prevent similar incidents in the future. CLI commands can be used to capture and analyze forensic data, conduct post-incident interviews, and document findings and recommendations for future enhancements. For example, organizations can use CLI commands to collect memory dumps, analyze network traffic logs, and review security configurations to identify vulnerabilities and weaknesses exploited during the incident. Incident response planning is an iterative process that requires regular review, testing, and refinement to ensure effectiveness and adaptability to evolving threats and technologies. CLI commands can be used to automate incident response exercises, simulate attack scenarios, and evaluate the readiness of incident response teams and procedures. For example, organizations can use CLI scripts to orchestrate tabletop exercises, simulate phishing attacks, and assess the effectiveness of incident detection and response capabilities. By incorporating CLI commands into incident response planning, organizations can streamline incident response processes, enhance collaboration among response teams, and improve the effectiveness of incident detection, containment, and recovery efforts.

Cloud-based disaster recovery solutions have become increasingly popular among organizations seeking to protect their data and applications from potential disruptions and outages. CLI commands are often used to deploy and manage cloud-based disaster recovery solutions, enabling organizations to automate recovery processes, replicate data to off-site locations, and ensure business continuity in the event of a disaster. For example, in Amazon Web Services (AWS), organizations can use the AWS Command Line Interface (CLI) to configure disaster recovery services such as AWS Backup, AWS Disaster Recovery, and AWS Site Recovery, to replicate data and applications across regions and availability zones. Cloud-based disaster recovery solutions leverage the scalability and resilience of cloud infrastructure to provide cost-effective and reliable protection against a wide range of threats, including hardware failures, natural disasters, cyberattacks, and human errors. By storing data and running applications in the cloud, organizations can reduce the risk of data loss and downtime, improve recovery times, and minimize the impact of disruptions on business operations. CLI commands can be used to automate disaster recovery processes, such as configuring replication settings, initiating failover procedures, and monitoring recovery progress.

For example, organizations can use AWS CLI commands to create backup plans, schedule backups, and restore data from backups stored in Amazon S3 or Amazon Glacier. One of the key advantages of cloud-based disaster recovery solutions is their flexibility and scalability, allowing organizations to scale resources up or down based on changing requirements and budget constraints.

CLI commands can be used to automate resource provisioning, scale compute and storage capacity, and optimize costs for disaster recovery workloads. For example, organizations can use AWS CLI commands to automate the deployment of EC2 instances, EBS volumes, and other resources needed for disaster recovery, and use AWS Cost Explorer to analyze and optimize costs associated with running disaster recovery workloads in the cloud. Cloud-based disaster recovery solutions also offer simplified management and monitoring capabilities, enabling organizations to centrally manage and monitor recovery processes across multiple locations and environments. CLI commands can be used to configure monitoring alerts, track recovery metrics, and generate reports on recovery status and performance. For example, organizations can use AWS CLI commands to configure CloudWatch alarms to monitor resource utilization, set up SNS notifications for critical events, and create CloudWatch dashboards to visualize recovery metrics and trends.

To deploy a cloud-based disaster recovery solution, organizations must first assess their business requirements, identify critical applications and data, and define recovery objectives and priorities. CLI commands can be used to automate the assessment process, collect inventory data, and analyze dependencies and interdependencies between applications and systems. For example, organizations can use AWS CLI commands to scan their environments, identify critical workloads, and prioritize them for replication and failover. Once the requirements are defined, organizations can select and configure the appropriate cloud-based disaster recovery services and solutions to meet their needs. CLI commands can be used to provision resources, configure replication settings, and test failover procedures to ensure readiness for disaster recovery scenarios. For example, organizations can use AWS CLI commands to configure AWS Backup policies, create cross-region replication jobs, and conduct failover tests using AWS Disaster Recovery and AWS Site Recovery services. Once the cloud-based disaster recovery solution is deployed and configured, organizations must regularly test and validate their recovery processes to ensure they meet recovery objectives and compliance requirements. CLI commands can be used to automate testing procedures, simulate disaster scenarios, and validate recovery plans. For example, organizations can use AWS CLI commands to automate the execution of recovery scripts, validate data integrity, and verify application functionality after failover. By leveraging CLI commands and cloud-based disaster recovery solutions, organizations can enhance their resilience to disruptions, improve recovery times, and ensure business continuity in the face of unforeseen events.

Chapter 10: Emerging Trends and Future Directions in Cloud Security

Edge computing and IoT security are intertwined topics at the forefront of modern technology, addressing the challenges and opportunities presented by the proliferation of Internet of Things (IoT) devices and the decentralization of computing resources. CLI commands are increasingly utilized to deploy and manage security measures in edge computing environments, allowing organizations to protect IoT devices, data, and networks from potential threats and vulnerabilities. Edge computing involves processing data near the source of data generation, rather than relying on centralized data centers, to reduce latency, improve performance, and enable real-time decision-making. CLI commands can be used to deploy edge computing infrastructure, such as edge servers, gateways, and edge devices, and configure security controls to protect data and applications at the edge. For example, organizations can use CLI commands to provision and configure edge servers and gateways in distributed locations, set up VPN connections for secure communication, and enforce access controls to restrict unauthorized access to edge resources. Security is a primary concern in edge computing environments, given the distributed nature of resources and the diversity of IoT devices connected to the network. CLI commands can be used to implement security measures such as encryption, authentication, and access controls to safeguard data in transit and at rest. For example, organizations can use CLI commands to configure encryption protocols such as Transport Layer Security (TLS) for secure communication between edge devices and cloud services, and implement access control lists (ACLs) to restrict access to sensitive data stored on edge servers. IoT devices, which are integral components of edge computing ecosystems, present unique security challenges due to their resource constraints, limited processing power, and susceptibility to attacks. CLI commands can be used to secure IoT devices by updating firmware, configuring firewalls, and implementing security policies to protect against common threats such as malware, botnets, and denial-of-service (DoS) attacks. For example, organizations can use CLI commands to deploy intrusion detection and prevention systems (IDPS) on edge devices, monitor network traffic for suspicious activity, and block malicious traffic using firewall rules. As edge computing environments continue to evolve and expand, organizations must adopt a holistic approach to IoT security that addresses the entire lifecycle of IoT devices, from provisioning and deployment to decommissioning. CLI commands can be used to automate device management tasks such as device registration, provisioning, and configuration management, ensuring that IoT devices are properly configured and maintained throughout their lifecycle. For example, organizations can use CLI commands to enroll IoT devices in device management platforms, assign device profiles based on security requirements, and remotely update device firmware and software using over-the-air (OTA) updates. Compliance with industry regulations and standards is another important aspect of IoT security in edge computing environments. CLI commands can be used to audit edge computing infrastructure for compliance with regulations such as the General Data Protection Regulation (GDPR), the Health Insurance Portability and Accountability Act (HIPAA), and the Payment Card Industry Data Security Standard (PCI DSS). For example, organizations can use CLI commands to generate compliance reports, conduct vulnerability scans, and remediate non-compliant configurations to ensure adherence to regulatory requirements. In conclusion, edge computing and IoT security are essential components of modern IT infrastructure, enabling organizations to harness the power of distributed computing while protecting sensitive data and assets from cyber threats. By leveraging CLI commands to deploy and manage security measures in edge computing environments, organizations can enhance the resilience, reliability, and security of their IoT deployments, ensuring that they remain protected in the face of evolving threats and vulnerabilities.

AI and machine learning are revolutionizing the field of cloud security, offering advanced capabilities for threat detection, risk analysis, and incident response. CLI commands play a crucial role in deploying and managing AI and machine learning solutions in cloud security, enabling organizations to automate security operations, analyze vast amounts of data, and identify anomalous behavior indicative of security threats. For example, in Amazon Web Services (AWS), organizations can use the AWS Command Line Interface (CLI) to configure and deploy machine learning models for anomaly detection, intrusion detection, and predictive analytics. AI and machine learning algorithms can analyze patterns and trends in network traffic, user behavior, and system logs to detect deviations from normal activity that may indicate potential security breaches or cyber attacks. CLI commands can be used to collect and preprocess data, train machine learning models, and deploy trained models to production environments for real-time detection and response. For example, organizations can use CLI commands to ingest log data from cloud services, preprocess data using tools like AWS Glue or Apache Spark, and train machine learning models using frameworks such as TensorFlow or PyTorch. Once trained, machine learning models can be deployed as endpoints or services using CLI commands to analyze incoming data streams, classify events, and generate alerts or notifications for security incidents. For example, organizations can use AWS CLI commands to deploy machine learning models as AWS Lambda functions, AWS SageMaker endpoints, or AWS IoT Core rules to analyze telemetry data from IoT devices and detect anomalies indicative of security threats. AI and machine learning can also enhance threat intelligence and security analytics by identifying emerging threats, correlating events across multiple sources, and prioritizing alerts based on risk and impact. CLI commands can be used to integrate AI and machine learning capabilities with existing security information and event management (SIEM) systems, threat intelligence platforms, and security orchestration, automation, and response (SOAR) tools. For example, organizations can use CLI commands to ingest threat intelligence feeds, enrich security events with contextual information, and automate incident response actions based on machine learning predictions. In addition to threat detection and response, AI and machine learning can improve security posture through proactive risk management and compliance monitoring. CLI commands can be used to analyze historical data, identify security trends and patterns, and forecast potential security risks or vulnerabilities. For example, organizations can use CLI commands to analyze audit logs, identify common security misconfigurations, and generate recommendations for remediation using machine learning algorithms. AI and machine learning can also automate compliance assessments by analyzing cloud configurations against industry standards and regulatory requirements. CLI commands can be used to scan cloud resources for compliance violations, generate compliance reports, and enforce security policies using machine learning-driven automation. For example, organizations can use CLI commands to deploy AWS Config rules, AWS Security Hub findings, or AWS Trusted Advisor checks to continuously monitor cloud configurations for compliance with frameworks such as the NIST Cybersecurity Framework or the Center for Internet Security (CIS) benchmarks. In conclusion, AI and machine learning are transforming cloud security by enabling organizations to detect, respond to, and mitigate security threats more effectively. By leveraging CLI commands to deploy and manage AI and machine learning solutions in cloud environments, organizations can enhance their security posture, reduce the risk of data breaches, and ensure compliance with regulatory requirements and industry standards.

BOOK 2

NAVIGATING NIST GUIDELINES IMPLEMENTING CLOUD SECURITY BEST PRACTICES FOR INTERMEDIATE USERS

ROB BOTWRIGHT

Chapter 1: Understanding NIST Guidelines for Cloud Security

NIST Special Publications (SPs) encompass a wide range of documents that provide guidance, recommendations, and best practices for various aspects of information security and technology. These publications are developed by the National Institute of Standards and Technology (NIST), a non-regulatory agency of the United States Department of Commerce, with the aim of promoting cybersecurity and improving the security and resilience of information systems. CLI commands can be utilized to access and download NIST SPs from the NIST website, enabling organizations to stay informed about the latest security standards and guidelines. For example, individuals can use CLI commands to navigate the NIST website, search for specific SPs using keywords or publication numbers, and download the desired documents in PDF or other formats for reference and implementation. NIST SPs cover a wide range of topics, including risk management, cryptography, cybersecurity frameworks, secure software development, and incident response, among others. Each SP is meticulously researched and developed by experts in the field, drawing upon industry best practices, public feedback, and collaboration with stakeholders to ensure relevance and effectiveness. CLI commands can also be employed to automate the retrieval and parsing of information from NIST SPs, facilitating the integration of NIST guidelines into organizational policies and procedures. For example, organizations can use CLI commands to extract specific sections or recommendations from SPs, convert them into machine-readable formats such as JSON or XML, and integrate them into security assessment tools, compliance dashboards, or security information and event management (SIEM) systems for ongoing monitoring and enforcement. NIST SPs are widely recognized and adopted by government agencies, private sector organizations, academia, and international entities as authoritative sources of security guidance and standards. Compliance with NIST SPs is often mandated or recommended by regulatory bodies, industry associations, and contractual agreements, making them essential references for organizations seeking to achieve and maintain cybersecurity maturity. CLI commands can be employed to automate compliance assessments against NIST SPs, enabling organizations to evaluate their security posture, identify gaps and deficiencies, and prioritize remediation efforts. For example, organizations can use CLI commands to parse SPs for specific controls or requirements, map them to existing security controls or frameworks such as the NIST Cybersecurity Framework (CSF) or ISO/IEC 27001, and generate compliance reports or scorecards to demonstrate adherence to NIST guidelines. NIST SPs are regularly updated and revised to address emerging threats, technological advancements, and changes in regulatory landscape. CLI commands can be utilized to monitor changes to SPs, subscribe to notification services, and receive alerts when new versions or revisions are published. For example, individuals can use CLI commands to query the NIST website or API for updates to SPs, compare changes between versions, and assess the impact on existing security programs or initiatives. In summary, NIST Special Publications are invaluable resources for organizations seeking to enhance their cybersecurity posture and protect their information assets. CLI commands provide a convenient and efficient means of accessing, analyzing, and applying NIST guidelines, enabling organizations to stay ahead of evolving threats and maintain compliance with industry standards and best practices.

NIST cloud security guidelines are founded on several key principles designed to ensure the confidentiality, integrity, and availability of data and resources in cloud environments. CLI commands are instrumental in implementing these principles, enabling organizations to configure and manage cloud security controls effectively. One fundamental principle emphasized by NIST is the importance of risk management in cloud security. Organizations must assess and prioritize risks associated with cloud adoption, considering factors such as data sensitivity, compliance requirements, and potential threats. CLI commands can facilitate risk assessments by automating the collection and analysis of data, generating risk scores, and identifying mitigation strategies. For example, organizations can use CLI commands to query cloud service provider APIs for information about data storage locations, encryption settings, and access controls, and use this data to assess the risk of data exposure or unauthorized access. Another key principle of NIST cloud security guidelines is the need for strong authentication and access controls to protect cloud resources from unauthorized access. CLI commands can be used to configure identity and access management (IAM) policies, enforce multi-factor authentication (MFA), and monitor user activity to detect suspicious behavior. For example, organizations can use CLI commands to create IAM roles, assign permissions to users and groups, and enable MFA for privileged accounts to prevent unauthorized access to sensitive data and applications. Data encryption is also a core principle of NIST cloud security guidelines, ensuring that data is protected both in transit and at rest. CLI commands can be used to configure encryption settings for data stored in cloud storage services, databases, and communication channels. For example, organizations can use CLI commands to enable encryption at rest for Amazon S3 buckets, configure SSL/TLS encryption for Amazon RDS instances, and encrypt data before transmitting it over the network using VPN or IPsec protocols. Another important principle outlined by NIST is the need for continuous monitoring and logging to detect and respond to security incidents in cloud environments. CLI commands can be used to configure monitoring tools, set up alarms and notifications, and analyze log data to identify anomalous behavior indicative of security threats. For example, organizations can use CLI commands to enable CloudTrail logging in AWS, configure CloudWatch alarms to alert on specific security events, and analyze VPC flow logs to detect unauthorized network traffic. Additionally, NIST emphasizes the importance of data governance and compliance in cloud security, requiring organizations to establish policies and procedures for data classification, retention, and disposal. CLI commands can be used to enforce data governance policies, audit cloud configurations for compliance with regulatory requirements, and generate compliance reports. For example, organizations can use CLI commands to tag data with metadata attributes indicating sensitivity levels, automate data retention policies using lifecycle rules in cloud storage services, and conduct compliance assessments against industry standards such as PCI DSS or HIPAA. Finally, NIST cloud security guidelines advocate for a shared responsibility model, where both cloud service providers and customers are responsible for different aspects of security. CLI commands can be used to configure security controls provided by cloud service providers, such as network security groups, firewalls, and encryption services, as well as to implement additional security measures at the customer's end. For example, organizations can use CLI commands to configure AWS security groups to restrict inbound and outbound traffic, deploy third-party security appliances in virtual private clouds (VPCs), and integrate cloud security controls with on-premises security tools using APIs and command-line interfaces. In conclusion, NIST cloud security guidelines provide a comprehensive framework for securing cloud environments, based on key principles such as risk management, authentication and access control, data encryption, continuous monitoring, data governance, compliance, and shared responsibility. CLI commands play a crucial role in implementing these principles, enabling organizations to configure and manage cloud security controls effectively and mitigate risks associated with cloud adoption.

Chapter 2: Evaluating Cloud Security Maturity Levels

Maturity model frameworks for cloud security provide organizations with a structured approach to assessing and improving their security posture in cloud environments. CLI commands can be instrumental in deploying and managing maturity model frameworks, enabling organizations to automate assessment processes, track progress, and implement security controls effectively. One widely adopted maturity model framework is the Cloud Security Alliance (CSA) Cloud Controls Matrix (CCM), which provides a comprehensive set of security controls mapped to leading security standards and regulations. CLI commands can be used to download the CCM, import it into security assessment tools, and automate the evaluation of cloud security controls against organizational requirements. For example, organizations can use CLI commands to clone the CCM repository from GitHub, convert it into a machine-readable format such as JSON or YAML, and integrate it with security automation tools such as AWS Config or Azure Policy. Another popular maturity model framework is the NIST Cybersecurity Framework

(CSF), which offers a risk-based approach to managing cybersecurity risk. CLI commands can be used to access and deploy the CSF, enabling organizations to assess their current cybersecurity posture, identify gaps and weaknesses, and prioritize improvements based on risk. For example, organizations can use CLI commands to download the CSF from the NIST website, import it into a governance, risk, and compliance (GRC) platform, and automate the assessment of cybersecurity controls using predefined assessment templates. The Center for Internet Security (CIS) also offers a maturity model framework for cloud security, known as the CIS Controls for Cloud. CLI commands can be used to download the CIS Controls for Cloud, configure security benchmarks, and assess cloud security configurations against CIS best practices. For example, organizations can use CLI commands to retrieve the CIS Controls for Cloud from the CIS website, import them into a configuration management tool such as Terraform or Ansible, and automate the deployment of security controls across cloud environments. The maturity model framework provides organizations with a roadmap for advancing their security capabilities over time, moving from ad-hoc and reactive approaches to proactive and mature security practices. CLI commands can be used to track progress along the maturity model, assess maturity levels, and prioritize initiatives for improvement. For example, organizations can use CLI commands to query security assessment tools for maturity scores, generate maturity reports, and visualize trends and patterns using dashboards and analytics tools. As organizations progress through the maturity model framework, they can achieve higher levels of security maturity, improve resilience to cyber threats, and enhance their ability to protect sensitive data and assets in cloud environments. CLI commands can be used to automate the implementation of security controls, enforce security policies, and monitor compliance with regulatory requirements. For example, organizations can use CLI commands to deploy security automation scripts, enforce security configurations using infrastructure as code (IaC) tools, and monitor cloud environments for deviations from security baselines using continuous monitoring tools. In conclusion, maturity model frameworks for cloud security offer organizations a structured approach to improving their security posture and managing cybersecurity risk in cloud environments. CLI commands play a crucial role in deploying and managing maturity model frameworks, enabling organizations to automate security assessments, track progress, and implement security controls effectively. By leveraging maturity model frameworks and CLI commands, organizations can enhance their security capabilities, reduce the risk of data breaches, and ensure compliance with regulatory requirements and industry standards. Assessing organizational cloud security maturity is a critical step in understanding an organization's readiness to manage security risks in cloud environments. CLI commands can play a significant role in conducting such assessments, enabling organizations to automate data collection, analysis, and reporting processes. One approach to assessing cloud security maturity is to use maturity model frameworks such as the Cloud Security Alliance (CSA) Cloud Controls Matrix (CCM). CLI commands can be utilized to download the CCM framework, extract relevant controls, and assess their implementation status across various cloud services. For instance, organizations can use CLI commands to clone the CCM repository from GitHub, parse the controls using scripting languages like Python, and query cloud service provider APIs to gather configuration data for assessment. Another method for assessing cloud security maturity is to conduct security posture assessments using cloud security assessment tools. CLI commands can be employed to deploy and configure these tools, initiate security assessments, and retrieve assessment results for analysis. For example, organizations can use CLI commands to deploy tools like AWS Security Hub or Azure Security Center, configure assessment policies, and run assessments across cloud accounts and subscriptions. Additionally, organizations can assess cloud security maturity by conducting audits and compliance assessments against industry standards and regulatory requirements. CLI commands can facilitate these assessments by automating audit procedures, generating compliance reports, and identifying areas of non-compliance. For instance, organizations can use CLI commands to deploy compliance scanning tools such as AWS Config or Azure Policy, configure compliance rulesets based on standards like PCI DSS or GDPR, and generate compliance reports using CLI commands to extract and format assessment results. Moreover, organizations can assess cloud security maturity by evaluating their incident response capabilities in cloud environments. CLI commands can aid in simulating security incidents, testing incident response procedures, and identifying areas for improvement. For example, organizations can use CLI commands to deploy and configure incident response automation tools such as AWS Incident Manager or Azure Sentinel, orchestrate incident response workflows, and conduct tabletop exercises to validate incident response plans. Another aspect of assessing cloud security maturity is evaluating the effectiveness of security awareness and training programs. CLI commands can support this evaluation by automating the distribution of security awareness materials, tracking employee participation in training activities, and measuring the impact of training initiatives. For instance, organizations can use CLI commands to deploy learning management systems (LMS) in cloud environments, enroll employees in security awareness courses, and generate reports on training completion rates and performance metrics. Additionally, organizations can assess cloud security maturity by evaluating the integration of security into DevOps practices and processes. CLI commands can assist in this assessment by automating security testing, integrating security controls into CI/CD pipelines, and monitoring code repositories for security vulnerabilities. For example, organizations can use CLI commands to deploy DevSecOps tools such as AWS CodePipeline or Azure DevOps, configure security scanning and testing tasks within pipelines, and analyze pipeline logs and metrics to assess security posture. In summary, assessing organizational cloud security maturity is essential for identifying strengths, weaknesses, and areas for improvement in managing security risks in cloud environments. CLI commands can streamline and automate various aspects of the assessment process, enabling organizations to conduct comprehensive and efficient evaluations of their cloud security posture. By leveraging CLI commands in conjunction with established assessment methodologies and frameworks, organizations can enhance their ability to protect sensitive data and assets in the cloud and mitigate security risks effectively.

Chapter 3: Selecting and Implementing Cloud Security Controls

Identifying appropriate security controls is a crucial aspect of developing an effective cybersecurity strategy for organizations operating in the digital age. CLI commands can be invaluable in this process, facilitating the identification, implementation, and management of security controls across various technology platforms and environments. One method for identifying security controls is to conduct a risk assessment to evaluate the threats, vulnerabilities, and potential impacts facing an organization's assets and operations. CLI commands can be utilized to automate risk assessments, gather data from various sources, and analyze risk factors to prioritize control implementation efforts. For instance, organizations can use CLI commands to query vulnerability scanners, log management systems, and asset inventories to collect data on security threats and vulnerabilities, and use scripting languages like Python or PowerShell to analyze this data and generate risk scores. Another approach for identifying security controls is to leverage industry standards and frameworks such as the NIST Cybersecurity Framework (CSF) or ISO/IEC 27001. CLI commands can be employed to access and interpret these standards, extract relevant control requirements, and map them to the organization's specific security needs and objectives. For example, organizations can use CLI commands to download the NIST CSF from the NIST website, parse the framework using scripting tools, and customize control mappings based on organizational risk assessments and security policies. Additionally, organizations can identify security controls by conducting security assessments and audits to evaluate existing security measures and identify gaps or deficiencies. CLI commands can facilitate these assessments by automating data collection, analysis, and reporting processes. For instance, organizations can use CLI commands to deploy vulnerability scanning tools, configuration management systems, and compliance auditing tools, and use scripting languages to automate assessment tasks and generate actionable insights from assessment results. Furthermore, organizations can identify security controls by considering regulatory requirements and industry best practices relevant to their sector and geographic location. CLI commands can assist in interpreting regulatory mandates, extracting control requirements, and aligning them with organizational policies and objectives. For example, organizations subject to the General Data Protection Regulation (GDPR) can use CLI commands to access the regulation text, extract data protection requirements, and develop control frameworks to ensure compliance with GDPR provisions. Moreover, organizations can identify security controls by considering emerging threats and evolving technology trends that may impact their security posture. CLI commands can help organizations stay informed about emerging threats and trends, gather threat intelligence data, and adjust security controls accordingly. For example, organizations can use CLI commands to access threat intelligence feeds, analyze threat data using machine learning algorithms, and deploy automated response mechanisms to mitigate emerging threats in real-time. In summary, identifying appropriate security controls is a critical step in developing a robust cybersecurity strategy that addresses the evolving threat landscape and protects organizational assets and operations. CLI commands offer a versatile and efficient means of identifying, implementing, and managing security controls, enabling organizations to stay ahead of cyber threats and maintain a strong security posture in today's digital world. By leveraging CLI commands in conjunction with established security frameworks, standards, and best practices, organizations can enhance their resilience to cyber attacks and safeguard their data and systems against unauthorized access, disclosure, and exploitation.

Implementing cloud security controls requires careful planning, execution, and ongoing management to effectively mitigate risks and protect organizational assets and data in cloud environments. CLI commands play a crucial role in deploying and managing these controls, offering automation, scalability, and efficiency. One best practice for implementing cloud security controls is to start with a comprehensive risk assessment to identify the organization's unique security requirements, threats, and vulnerabilities. CLI commands can automate data collection and analysis processes, enabling organizations to assess risks across cloud services and prioritize control implementation efforts. For example, organizations can use CLI commands to query cloud service provider APIs for configuration data, scan cloud resources for security vulnerabilities, and analyze log data to identify potential threats. Another best practice is to leverage cloud-native security services and features provided by cloud service providers, such as AWS, Azure, or Google Cloud. CLI commands can be used to configure these services, enabling organizations to implement security controls such as encryption, access control, and monitoring seamlessly. For example, organizations can use CLI commands to deploy AWS Security Groups, Azure Security Center policies, or Google Cloud Identity and Access Management (IAM) roles to enforce security policies and protect cloud resources from unauthorized access or misuse. Additionally, organizations should implement network security controls to segment and isolate cloud resources, reducing the risk of lateral movement and unauthorized access within cloud environments. CLI commands can automate the deployment of network security controls such as virtual private clouds (VPCs), network access control lists (ACLs), and security groups, enabling organizations to enforce network segmentation and control traffic flows effectively. For example, organizations can use CLI commands to create VPCs, define subnets, and configure security groups to restrict inbound and outbound traffic based on source IP addresses, port numbers, and protocols. Furthermore, organizations should implement identity and access management (IAM) controls to enforce the principle of least privilege and ensure that only authorized users and applications have access to cloud resources. CLI commands can be used to create IAM policies, roles, and permissions, enabling organizations to grant access rights based on job roles, responsibilities, and business requirements. For example, organizations can use CLI commands to create IAM users, assign them to groups, and define policies that grant access to specific cloud services and resources. Another best practice is to implement encryption controls to protect data at rest and in transit within cloud environments. CLI commands can automate the deployment of encryption services and features, enabling organizations to encrypt data using strong cryptographic algorithms and manage encryption keys securely. For example, organizations can use CLI commands to enable server-side encryption for cloud storage buckets, configure SSL/TLS encryption for network traffic, and manage encryption keys using cloud-based key management services. Additionally, organizations should implement logging and monitoring controls to detect and respond to security incidents in real-time. CLI commands can be used to configure logging and monitoring services, enabling organizations to collect, analyze, and correlate security events and alerts from multiple sources. For example, organizations can use CLI commands to enable CloudTrail logging in AWS, configure CloudWatch alarms to alert on specific security events, and integrate with third-party security information and event management (SIEM) systems using CLI commands to forward logs and events for analysis and correlation. In conclusion, implementing cloud security controls requires a holistic approach that encompasses risk assessment, cloud-native security services, network security, IAM, encryption, logging, and monitoring. CLI commands offer a powerful toolset for deploying and managing these controls efficiently and effectively, enabling organizations to protect their cloud environments from a wide range of security threats and vulnerabilities. By following best practices and leveraging CLI commands, organizations can enhance their cloud security posture, reduce the risk of data breaches, and ensure compliance with regulatory requirements and industry standards.

Chapter 4: Risk Management Strategies in Cloud Environments

Risk assessment methodologies for cloud environments are essential for identifying, analyzing, and mitigating security risks inherent in cloud computing. CLI commands play a crucial role in deploying these methodologies, automating data collection, analysis, and reporting processes. One commonly used risk assessment methodology is the NIST Risk Management Framework (RMF), which provides a structured approach to managing risks in cloud environments. CLI commands can be used to access and deploy the NIST RMF, enabling organizations to assess risks systematically and prioritize mitigation efforts. For example, organizations can use CLI commands to download the NIST RMF publication, extract risk assessment templates, and customize them based on their specific cloud environment and security requirements. Another widely adopted risk assessment methodology is the ISO/IEC 27005 standard, which offers guidelines for conducting information security risk assessments. CLI commands can assist in implementing the ISO/IEC

27005 methodology, enabling organizations to identify assets, threats, vulnerabilities, and controls relevant to cloud security. For instance, organizations can use CLI commands to access the ISO/IEC 27005 standard, extract risk assessment frameworks, and adapt them to assess risks associated with cloud services and deployments. Additionally, organizations can leverage cloud-specific risk assessment methodologies developed by industry organizations and cloud service providers. CLI commands can facilitate the deployment of these methodologies, enabling organizations to assess risks unique to cloud environments effectively. For example, organizations can use CLI commands to access risk assessment tools provided by cloud service providers such as AWS, Azure, or Google Cloud, and integrate them into their risk management processes. Furthermore, organizations can develop custom risk assessment methodologies tailored to their specific cloud deployments and security requirements. CLI commands can automate the deployment of these methodologies, enabling organizations to assess risks comprehensively and proactively. For instance, organizations can use CLI commands to create risk assessment scripts, deploy them across cloud environments, and collect data on assets, configurations, and security controls using cloud APIs. Moreover, organizations can leverage threat intelligence feeds and risk scoring algorithms to enhance their risk assessment methodologies. CLI commands can be used to integrate threat intelligence feeds into risk assessment tools, enabling organizations to identify emerging threats and assess their potential impact on cloud security. For example, organizations can use CLI commands to query threat intelligence APIs, extract threat data, and correlate it with risk assessment data to prioritize mitigation efforts. Additionally, organizations can use CLI commands to deploy risk scoring algorithms that assign risk scores to assets, vulnerabilities, and threats based on their severity and likelihood of exploitation. In conclusion, risk assessment methodologies for cloud environments are essential for identifying, analyzing, and mitigating security risks associated with cloud computing. CLI commands offer a versatile and efficient means of deploying these methodologies, enabling organizations to assess risks comprehensively, prioritize mitigation efforts, and enhance their overall security posture in the cloud. By leveraging CLI commands in conjunction with established risk assessment frameworks and methodologies, organizations can proactively identify and address security risks, protect sensitive data and assets, and maintain compliance with regulatory requirements and industry standards.

Mitigation strategies for cloud security risks are essential for organizations seeking to protect their data, applications, and infrastructure in cloud environments. CLI commands play a vital role in deploying and managing these strategies, offering automation, scalability, and efficiency. One effective mitigation strategy is to implement strong access controls and authentication mechanisms to prevent unauthorized access to cloud resources. CLI commands can be used to configure identity and access management (IAM) policies, roles, and permissions, ensuring that only authorized users and applications have access to sensitive data and resources. For example, organizations can use CLI commands to create IAM users, assign them to groups, and define policies that restrict access based on job roles and responsibilities. Additionally, organizations should encrypt data at rest and in transit to protect it from unauthorized access and interception. CLI commands can automate the deployment of encryption services and features, enabling organizations to encrypt data using strong cryptographic algorithms and manage encryption keys securely. For instance, organizations can use

CLI commands to enable server-side encryption for cloud storage buckets, configure SSL/TLS encryption for network traffic, and manage encryption keys using cloud-based key management services. Another mitigation strategy is to implement network segmentation and isolation to prevent lateral movement and limit the impact of security breaches. CLI commands can be used to deploy network security controls such as virtual private clouds (VPCs), network access control lists (ACLs), and security groups, enabling organizations to enforce network segmentation and control traffic flows effectively. For example, organizations can use CLI commands to create VPCs, define subnets, and configure security groups to restrict inbound and outbound traffic based on source IP addresses, port numbers, and protocols. Furthermore, organizations should regularly patch and update cloud resources to address known vulnerabilities and security weaknesses. CLI commands can automate the patch management process, enabling organizations to scan cloud environments for outdated software and apply patches automatically. For instance, organizations can use CLI commands to deploy patch management tools, schedule automated scans, and remediate vulnerabilities by applying patches using scripting languages or configuration management tools. Additionally, organizations should implement logging and monitoring controls to detect and respond to security incidents in real-time. CLI commands can be used to configure logging and monitoring services, enabling organizations to collect, analyze, and correlate security events and alerts from multiple sources. For example, organizations can use CLI commands to enable logging for cloud services, configure log aggregation and retention policies, and set up alerts to notify security teams of suspicious activities or anomalies. Moreover, organizations should conduct regular security assessments and audits to identify gaps and weaknesses in their cloud security posture. CLI commands can automate data collection, analysis, and reporting processes, enabling organizations to assess risks comprehensively and prioritize mitigation efforts effectively. For example, organizations can use CLI commands to deploy vulnerability scanning tools, configuration management systems, and compliance auditing tools, and use scripting languages to automate assessment tasks and generate actionable insights from assessment results. In conclusion, mitigation strategies for cloud security risks are essential for organizations to protect their data, applications, and infrastructure in cloud environments. CLI commands offer a powerful toolset for deploying and managing these strategies efficiently and effectively, enabling organizations to mitigate risks, reduce the likelihood of security breaches, and maintain a strong security posture in the cloud. By leveraging CLI commands in conjunction with established security best practices and frameworks, organizations can enhance their resilience to cyber threats, safeguard sensitive data and assets, and ensure compliance with regulatory requirements and industry standards.

Chapter 5: Advanced Identity and Access Management Techniques

Multi-factor authentication (MFA) is a critical security measure in cloud environments, providing an additional layer of protection beyond traditional password-based authentication. CLI commands are instrumental in deploying and managing MFA solutions, offering automation and efficiency in securing access to cloud resources. One popular MFA method is Time-based One-Time Password (TOTP), which generates temporary codes that users must provide along with their passwords to authenticate. CLI commands can be used to deploy TOTP-based MFA solutions, such as Google Authenticator or Authy, by configuring IAM policies and enabling MFA for IAM users. For example, organizations can use AWS CLI commands to enable MFA for IAM users by updating their user policies to require MFA authentication. Another common MFA method is SMS-based authentication, which sends one-time codes to users' mobile phones via SMS. CLI commands can automate the setup of SMS-based MFA, integrating with third-party SMS gateway services to deliver authentication codes.

For instance, organizations can use CLI commands to configure AWS SNS (Simple Notification Service) to send MFA codes to users' mobile phones via SMS, enhancing security for accessing AWS resources. Additionally, some MFA solutions leverage biometric authentication, such as fingerprint or facial recognition, to verify users' identities. CLI commands can facilitate the deployment of biometric MFA solutions by configuring authentication mechanisms and integrating with biometric authentication services. For example, organizations can use CLI commands to enable biometric MFA for Azure Active Directory users by configuring Windows Hello for Business settings and enabling biometric authentication policies. Furthermore, organizations can deploy hardware tokens as an MFA method, providing users with physical devices that generate authentication codes. CLI commands can automate the provisioning and management of hardware tokens, enabling organizations to distribute tokens to users and link them to their accounts securely. For instance, organizations can use CLI commands to integrate hardware token management solutions with identity management systems, enabling users to register and activate tokens for MFA authentication. Moreover, some cloud service providers offer built-in support for MFA, allowing organizations to enable MFA directly from their management consoles or CLI interfaces. For example, AWS provides CLI commands to enable MFA for IAM users, Azure offers PowerShell commands to enforce MFA for Azure AD users, and Google Cloud Platform supports enabling MFA for Google accounts through its admin console or CLI tools. Additionally, organizations should consider implementing adaptive authentication, which dynamically adjusts authentication requirements based on risk factors such as user location, device type, and behavior patterns. CLI commands can automate the configuration of adaptive authentication policies, enabling organizations to define rules and thresholds for triggering additional authentication challenges. For instance, organizations can use CLI commands to integrate adaptive authentication solutions with identity providers, enabling real-time risk assessment and adaptive response mechanisms. In conclusion, multi-factor authentication is a vital security measure in cloud environments, providing enhanced protection against unauthorized access and data breaches. CLI commands offer a powerful means of deploying and managing MFA solutions, enabling organizations to strengthen their security posture and safeguard sensitive data and resources in the cloud. By leveraging CLI commands to deploy MFA methods such as TOTP, SMS-based authentication, biometrics, hardware tokens, and adaptive authentication, organizations can effectively mitigate the risk of unauthorized access and enhance their overall security posture in the cloud.

Role-Based Access Control (RBAC) is a fundamental security principle that governs access to resources based on users' roles and responsibilities within an organization. CLI commands are instrumental in deploying and managing RBAC policies in cloud environments, providing automation and scalability in access management. One of the key advantages of RBAC is its ability to streamline access control by assigning permissions to roles rather than individual users. CLI commands can be used to create and manage roles, enabling organizations to define granular permissions that align with users' job functions and responsibilities. For example, in AWS, organizations can use the AWS CLI to create IAM roles with specific permissions using the aws iam create-role command, specifying the policies and permissions attached to each role. RBAC helps organizations enforce the principle of least privilege, ensuring that users have access only to the resources necessary for their roles. CLI commands facilitate the enforcement of least privilege by enabling organizations to restrict permissions based on users' roles and responsibilities. For instance, organizations can use CLI commands to attach IAM policies to roles, limiting access to specific AWS services, resources, or actions based on users' assigned roles. RBAC also simplifies access management by allowing organizations to centrally manage permissions across cloud environments. CLI commands can automate the synchronization of RBAC policies across multiple cloud platforms, ensuring consistency and compliance with security policies. For example, organizations can use CLI commands to export IAM policies from one AWS account and import them into another account using the AWS CLI's aws iam get-policy and aws iam put-policy commands. Additionally, RBAC enhances security by reducing the risk of unauthorized access and data breaches. CLI commands can be used to audit RBAC policies, identify unused or excessive permissions, and remediate security gaps proactively. For example, organizations can use CLI commands to generate IAM policy usage reports and analyze access patterns to identify anomalies or potential security threats. RBAC also facilitates segregation of duties, ensuring that critical tasks are divided among multiple roles to prevent conflicts of interest and mitigate the risk of insider threats. CLI commands enable organizations to enforce segregation of duties by defining role hierarchies and dependencies. For instance, organizations can use CLI commands to create IAM roles with specific trust relationships, allowing certain roles to assume other roles only under certain conditions. Moreover, RBAC supports scalability and agility in cloud environments by enabling organizations to adapt access controls dynamically to changing business requirements. CLI commands can automate the provisioning and deprovisioning of roles, enabling organizations to manage access efficiently as users join, move, or leave the organization. For example, organizations can use CLI commands to create IAM role templates and deploy them automatically using infrastructure-as-code (IaC) tools such as AWS CloudFormation or Terraform. In conclusion, Role-Based Access Control (RBAC) is a fundamental security principle that plays a crucial role in access management in cloud environments. CLI commands offer a powerful toolset for deploying and managing RBAC policies, enabling organizations to enforce least privilege, ensure consistency, enhance security, and support scalability in access management. By leveraging CLI commands to automate role provisioning, permissions management, and access auditing, organizations can strengthen their security posture and mitigate the risk of unauthorized access and data breaches in the cloud.

Chapter 6: Enhancing Data Protection in the Cloud

Role-Based Access Control (RBAC) is a fundamental security principle that governs access to resources based on users' roles and responsibilities within an organization. CLI commands are instrumental in deploying and managing RBAC policies in cloud environments, providing automation and scalability in access management. One of the key advantages of RBAC is its ability to streamline access control by assigning permissions to roles rather than individual users. CLI commands can be used to create and manage roles, enabling organizations to define granular permissions that align with users' job functions and responsibilities. For example, in AWS, organizations can use the AWS CLI to create IAM roles with specific permissions using the aws iam create-role command, specifying the policies and permissions attached to each role. RBAC helps organizations enforce the principle of least privilege, ensuring that users have access only to the resources necessary for their roles. CLI commands facilitate the enforcement of least privilege by enabling organizations to restrict permissions based on users' roles and responsibilities. For instance, organizations can use CLI commands to attach IAM policies to roles, limiting access to specific AWS services, resources, or actions based on users' assigned roles. RBAC also simplifies access management by allowing organizations to centrally manage permissions across cloud environments. CLI commands can automate the synchronization of RBAC policies across multiple cloud platforms, ensuring consistency and compliance with security policies. For example, organizations can use CLI commands to export IAM policies from one AWS account and import them into another account using the AWS CLI's aws iam get-policy and aws iam put-policy commands. Additionally, RBAC enhances security by reducing the risk of unauthorized access and data breaches. CLI commands can be used to audit RBAC policies, identify unused or excessive permissions, and remediate security gaps proactively. For example, organizations can use CLI commands to generate IAM policy usage reports and analyze access patterns to identify anomalies or potential security threats. RBAC also facilitates segregation of duties, ensuring that critical tasks are divided among multiple roles to prevent conflicts of interest and mitigate the risk of insider threats. CLI commands enable organizations to enforce segregation of duties by defining role hierarchies and dependencies. For instance, organizations can use CLI commands to create IAM roles with specific trust relationships, allowing certain roles to assume other roles only under certain conditions. Moreover, RBAC supports scalability and agility in cloud environments by enabling organizations to adapt access controls dynamically to changing business requirements. CLI commands can automate the provisioning and deprovisioning of roles, enabling organizations to manage access efficiently as users join, move, or leave the organization. For example, organizations can use CLI commands to create IAM role templates and deploy them automatically using infrastructure-as-code (IaC) tools such as AWS CloudFormation or Terraform. In conclusion, Role-Based Access Control (RBAC) is a fundamental security principle that plays a crucial role in access management in cloud environments. CLI commands offer a powerful toolset for deploying and managing RBAC policies, enabling organizations to enforce least privilege, ensure consistency, enhance security, and support scalability in access management. By leveraging CLI commands to automate role provisioning, permissions management, and access auditing, organizations can strengthen their security posture and mitigate the risk of unauthorized access and data breaches in the cloud. Data encryption protocols and standards are essential components of modern cybersecurity strategies, providing a robust framework for protecting sensitive information from unauthorized access and interception. CLI commands play a significant role in deploying and managing encryption protocols and standards in various computing environments, offering automation and efficiency in securing data. One widely used encryption protocol is the Transport Layer Security (TLS) protocol, which ensures secure communication over the internet by encrypting data transmitted between clients and servers. CLI commands can be used to configure TLS settings and certificates, enabling organizations to establish secure connections and protect data in transit. For example, organizations can use OpenSSL commands to generate SSL/TLS certificates, sign certificate requests, and configure TLS settings on web servers. Additionally, organizations can leverage the Advanced Encryption Standard (AES) for encrypting data at rest and in transit, providing strong cryptographic protection against brute-force attacks and unauthorized access. CLI commands can automate the deployment of AES encryption, enabling organizations to encrypt files, databases, and storage volumes efficiently. For instance, organizations can use the OpenSSL command-line tool to encrypt files using AES encryption algorithms with specified key lengths and encryption modes. Another important encryption standard is the Secure Sockets Layer (SSL) protocol, which encrypts data transmitted between clients and servers to prevent eavesdropping and tampering. CLI commands can be used to configure SSL settings and certificates, enabling organizations to secure their web applications and APIs effectively. For example, organizations can use the OpenSSL command-line tool to create SSL certificates, configure SSL/TLS settings on web servers, and test SSL connections for vulnerabilities. Moreover, organizations can deploy encryption protocols such as IPsec (Internet Protocol Security) to secure network communications between devices and endpoints. CLI commands can automate the configuration of IPsec tunnels and policies, enabling organizations to establish secure VPN connections and encrypt traffic between network segments. For instance, organizations can use the ipsec-tools package on Linux systems to configure IPsec tunnels, define security policies, and establish encrypted VPN connections between remote sites. Additionally, organizations can leverage encryption standards such as PGP (Pretty Good Privacy) for securing email communications and file transfers. CLI commands can facilitate the deployment of PGP encryption, enabling organizations to encrypt and decrypt messages, files, and attachments securely. For example, organizations can use the GnuPG command-line tool to generate PGP keys, encrypt email messages, and verify digital signatures. Furthermore, organizations can implement encryption standards such as SSH (Secure Shell) for securing remote access to servers and network devices. CLI commands can automate the configuration of SSH keys and settings, enabling organizations to authenticate users securely and encrypt data transmissions over SSH connections. For instance, organizations can use the ssh-keygen command-line tool to generate SSH key pairs, install public keys on remote servers, and configure SSH client and server settings for encryption and authentication. In conclusion, data encryption protocols and standards play a critical role in protecting sensitive information from unauthorized access and interception. CLI commands offer a versatile and efficient means of deploying and managing encryption technologies, enabling organizations to secure data in transit and at rest effectively. By leveraging CLI commands to configure TLS, AES, SSL, IPsec, PGP, SSH, and other encryption protocols, organizations can enhance their cybersecurity posture, mitigate the risk of data breaches, and ensure compliance with regulatory requirements and industry standards.

Chapter 7: Securing Cloud Networks: Advanced Considerations

Microsegmentation is a powerful network security technique that involves dividing a network into smaller, isolated segments to enhance security and control over traffic flows. CLI commands play a crucial role in deploying and managing microsegmentation in cloud networks, providing automation and efficiency in network configuration. One key benefit of microsegmentation is its ability to enforce granular access controls based on factors such as user identity, application type, or workload characteristics. CLI commands can be used to define security policies and access rules, enabling organizations to segment their cloud networks and restrict communication between different segments. For example, organizations can use the AWS CLI to configure security groups and network ACLs (Access Control Lists) to enforce microsegmentation in their AWS VPCs (Virtual Private Clouds). Additionally, microsegmentation helps organizations contain the lateral movement of threats within their networks by isolating workloads and applications from each other. CLI commands can automate the deployment of microsegmentation policies, enabling organizations to restrict communication between workloads and prevent the spread of malware or unauthorized access. For instance, organizations can use the Azure CLI to configure network security groups (NSGs) and apply them to subnets to enforce microsegmentation in their Azure virtual networks. Moreover, microsegmentation enhances visibility and control over network traffic, allowing organizations to monitor and analyze communication patterns between different segments. CLI commands can be used to deploy network monitoring and logging solutions, enabling organizations to capture and analyze traffic flows in real-time. For example, organizations can use the Google Cloud CLI to enable VPC Flow Logs and export them to monitoring and analysis tools for deeper insights into network activity. Furthermore, microsegmentation supports compliance efforts by providing a mechanism for enforcing security policies and regulatory requirements. CLI commands can automate the implementation of security controls and audit trails, enabling organizations to demonstrate compliance with industry standards and regulations. For instance, organizations can use the AWS CLI to configure

AWS Config rules to monitor compliance with security best practices and regulatory frameworks such as PCI DSS or HIPAA. Additionally, microsegmentation helps organizations reduce the blast radius of security incidents by isolating affected segments and preventing them from spreading to other parts of the network. CLI commands can automate incident response processes, enabling organizations to quarantine compromised workloads and contain security breaches effectively. For example, organizations can use the Kubernetes CLI (kubectl) to apply network policies that restrict communication between pods and limit the impact of compromised containers. Moreover, microsegmentation supports the adoption of zero trust security principles by treating every network communication as untrusted and verifying it before allowing access. CLI commands can facilitate the deployment of zero trust architectures, enabling organizations to implement strict access controls and authentication mechanisms. For instance, organizations can use the Terraform CLI to define infrastructure as code (IaC) templates that enforce zero trust policies and deploy them across cloud environments. In conclusion, microsegmentation is a valuable network security technique that enhances security, visibility, and control over cloud networks. CLI commands offer a powerful toolset for deploying and managing microsegmentation policies, enabling organizations to enforce access controls, contain threats, ensure compliance, and adopt zero trust security principles effectively. By leveraging CLI commands to automate network configuration and policy enforcement, organizations can strengthen their cybersecurity posture and mitigate the risk of data breaches and network attacks in cloud environments.

Advanced firewall configuration is essential for enhancing security and controlling network traffic in cloud environments, protecting organizations' assets from various cyber threats. CLI commands play a crucial role in deploying and managing advanced firewall configurations, offering automation and efficiency in network security management. One important aspect of advanced firewall configuration is the implementation of stateful packet inspection, which examines the state of each packet to determine whether it should be allowed or denied based on predefined rules. CLI commands can be used to configure stateful packet inspection rules, enabling organizations to inspect and filter traffic at the network level. For example, organizations can use iptables commands on Linux-based cloud instances to define stateful firewall rules that permit or block incoming and outgoing traffic based on source and destination IP addresses, ports, and protocols. Additionally, organizations can leverage advanced firewall features such as application-layer filtering to inspect and control traffic based on application-specific protocols and payloads. CLI commands can automate the deployment of application-layer firewall rules, enabling organizations to enforce granular access controls and protect against application-level attacks. For instance, organizations can use the Azure CLI to configure Azure Application Security Groups (ASGs) and define rules that filter traffic based on application-specific attributes such as URLs, HTTP headers, or payload content. Moreover, organizations can implement intrusion detection and prevention systems (IDPS) as part of their advanced firewall configuration to detect and block malicious activities in real-time. CLI commands can be used to deploy and manage IDPS rules and signatures, enabling organizations to detect and respond to security threats proactively. For example, organizations can use Snort CLI commands to update intrusion detection rules and enable packet inspection on network interfaces to identify and block suspicious traffic patterns. Furthermore, organizations can deploy network segmentation and isolation techniques as part of their advanced firewall configuration to limit the impact of security breaches and contain threats within specific network segments. CLI commands can automate the deployment of network segmentation rules, enabling organizations to partition their cloud networks and control traffic flows between segments. For instance, organizations can use the AWS CLI to configure security groups and network ACLs (Access Control Lists) to enforce network segmentation in their AWS VPCs (Virtual Private Clouds). Additionally, organizations can leverage advanced firewall features such as virtual firewalls and next-generation firewalls (NGFWs) to provide advanced threat protection and application visibility in cloud environments. CLI commands can be used to deploy and manage virtual firewall instances, enabling organizations to inspect and filter traffic at multiple layers of the OSI model. For example, organizations can use the Cisco ASA CLI to configure virtual firewall policies and security zones to enforce segmentation and protect against advanced threats. Moreover, organizations can implement centralized firewall management solutions to streamline the configuration and monitoring of firewall policies across distributed cloud environments. CLI commands can automate the deployment of centralized firewall management platforms, enabling organizations to define and enforce consistent security policies across multiple cloud regions and providers. For instance, organizations can use the Palo Alto Networks PAN-OS CLI to configure Panorama, a centralized firewall management platform, and deploy firewall policies to Palo Alto Networks firewalls deployed in various cloud environments. In conclusion, advanced firewall configuration is essential for securing cloud environments and protecting organizations' assets from cyber threats. CLI commands offer a powerful toolset for deploying and managing advanced firewall features, enabling organizations to enforce granular access controls, detect and block malicious activities, and contain threats effectively. By leveraging CLI commands to automate firewall configuration and management tasks, organizations can strengthen their cybersecurity posture and mitigate the risk of data breaches and network attacks in the cloud.

Chapter 8: Continuous Monitoring and Compliance Assurance

Implementing continuous monitoring tools is crucial for maintaining visibility and detecting security threats in dynamic IT environments. CLI commands play a significant role in deploying and managing continuous monitoring solutions, providing automation and efficiency in security operations. One widely used continuous monitoring tool is Security Information and Event Management (SIEM), which aggregates and analyzes log data from various sources to identify security incidents and anomalies. CLI commands can be used to deploy and configure SIEM agents on servers and endpoints, enabling organizations to collect and centralize log data for analysis. For example, organizations can use the Elastic Stack CLI to install and configure Beats agents on Linux servers to collect log data and ship it to an Elasticsearch cluster for analysis. Additionally, organizations can leverage log management platforms such as Splunk to index and search log data for security events and indicators of compromise. CLI commands can automate the deployment of Splunk forwarders on servers and workstations, enabling organizations to forward log data to a centralized Splunk instance for analysis. For instance, organizations can use the Splunk CLI to deploy universal forwarders on Windows systems to monitor event logs and forward them to a Splunk indexer for analysis. Moreover, organizations can implement network monitoring solutions such as Intrusion Detection Systems (IDS) and Network Traffic Analysis (NTA) tools to monitor network traffic for suspicious activities and security threats. CLI commands can be used to deploy and configure IDS/NTA sensors on network devices and servers, enabling organizations to analyze network traffic in real-time. For example, organizations can use the Suricata CLI to deploy IDS sensors on network gateways to monitor traffic for known attack signatures and behavioral anomalies. Additionally, organizations can leverage vulnerability management platforms such as Nessus to scan IT assets for security vulnerabilities and misconfigurations. CLI commands can automate the deployment of Nessus agents on servers and endpoints, enabling organizations to perform vulnerability scans and prioritize remediation efforts. For instance, organizations can use the Nessus CLI to deploy agents on Linux systems to perform credentialed scans and identify security vulnerabilities in software packages and configurations. Furthermore, organizations can implement file integrity monitoring (FIM) solutions to detect unauthorized changes to critical system files and configurations. CLI commands can be used to deploy FIM agents on servers and workstations, enabling organizations to monitor file integrity and detect suspicious modifications. For example, organizations can use the OSSEC CLI to deploy agents on Linux servers to monitor file systems for changes and trigger alerts for unauthorized modifications. Moreover, organizations can leverage cloud security posture management (CSPM) tools to assess and remediate security risks in cloud environments. CLI commands can automate the deployment of CSPM agents and APIs, enabling organizations to monitor cloud resources for misconfigurations and compliance violations. For instance, organizations can use the AWS CLI to deploy AWS Config agents on EC2 instances to monitor resource configurations and enforce security policies. In conclusion, implementing continuous monitoring tools is essential for maintaining visibility and detecting security threats in dynamic IT environments. CLI commands offer a powerful toolset for deploying and managing continuous monitoring solutions, enabling organizations to collect, analyze, and respond to security events effectively. By leveraging CLI commands to automate the deployment and configuration of monitoring agents and platforms, organizations can strengthen their cybersecurity posture and mitigate the risk of data breaches and security incidents.

Achieving compliance in dynamic cloud environments is a multifaceted challenge that requires organizations to navigate complex regulatory requirements and maintain adherence to industry standards. CLI commands play a crucial role in deploying and managing compliance frameworks, providing automation and efficiency in ensuring regulatory adherence. One of the first steps in achieving compliance is to understand the regulatory landscape and identify the relevant standards and requirements applicable to the organization's industry and geographic location. CLI commands can facilitate this process by enabling organizations to search for and retrieve regulatory documents and guidelines from authoritative sources. For example, organizations can use the curl command to retrieve regulatory documents from government websites or regulatory agencies' APIs. Additionally, organizations must assess their cloud infrastructure and applications against applicable compliance frameworks to identify gaps and areas of non-compliance. CLI commands can automate this assessment process by scanning cloud resources for misconfigurations and vulnerabilities. For instance, organizations can use the AWS CLI to run compliance checks against AWS Config rules or use cloud security assessment tools like CloudCheckr or AWS Trusted Advisor. Once organizations have identified compliance gaps, they must take remedial actions to address the issues and bring their cloud environments into compliance. CLI commands can be used to implement remediation measures such as applying security patches, configuring access controls, or encrypting data. For example, organizations can use the Azure CLI to apply security baselines or use Terraform scripts to automate the deployment of compliant infrastructure configurations. Moreover, organizations must establish robust monitoring and auditing mechanisms to track compliance status continuously and detect deviations from regulatory requirements. CLI commands can automate the deployment of monitoring agents and audit trails, enabling organizations to capture and analyze compliance-related data. For instance, organizations can use the GCP CLI to enable logging and monitoring features such as

Cloud Audit Logs or use third-party monitoring tools like Datadog or Splunk. Continuous compliance requires ongoing efforts to monitor, assess, and remediate compliance issues as cloud environments evolve. CLI commands can streamline these efforts by automating compliance checks and remediation workflows. For example, organizations can use the AWS Systems Manager Automation documents or Azure Automation Runbooks to create automated workflows for compliance monitoring and remediation. Additionally, organizations can leverage configuration management tools like Puppet or Chef to enforce compliance policies and configurations across cloud environments. Compliance certifications and attestations provide third-party validation of an organization's adherence to regulatory requirements and industry standards. CLI commands can assist organizations in preparing and documenting compliance audits by generating compliance reports and documentation. For example, organizations can use the AWS CLI to generate AWS Artifact reports or use cloud compliance management platforms like CloudCheckr or Fugue. Furthermore, organizations can leverage cloud-native compliance solutions and services offered by cloud providers to simplify compliance efforts. CLI commands can be used to deploy and configure these services, enabling organizations to leverage built-in compliance features and controls. For instance, organizations can use the Azure CLI to enable Azure Security Center or use AWS CLI to enable AWS Config Rules or AWS Security Hub. In conclusion, achieving compliance in dynamic cloud environments requires a holistic approach that combines regulatory knowledge, automation, and continuous monitoring. CLI commands offer a versatile and efficient means of deploying and managing compliance frameworks, enabling organizations to streamline compliance efforts and ensure adherence to regulatory requirements and industry standards. By leveraging CLI commands to automate compliance checks, remediation workflows, and audit preparations, organizations can strengthen their compliance posture and reduce the risk of regulatory violations and penalties.

Chapter 9: Incident Response Planning and Execution

Developing cloud-specific incident response plans is essential for organizations to effectively detect, respond to, and recover from security incidents in cloud environments. CLI commands play a crucial role in deploying and managing incident response plans, providing automation and efficiency in security incident management. One of the first steps in developing a cloud-specific incident response plan is to assess the organization's cloud infrastructure and identify potential security threats and vulnerabilities. CLI commands can facilitate this process by enabling organizations to scan cloud resources for misconfigurations and security risks. For example, organizations can use the AWS CLI to run vulnerability scans against their AWS assets using AWS Inspector or third-party vulnerability scanning tools. Additionally, organizations must define incident response procedures and workflows tailored to the unique characteristics of cloud environments. CLI commands can be used to create runbooks and playbooks that outline step-by-step instructions for responding to different types of security incidents. For instance, organizations can use Markdown syntax and version control systems like Git to maintain incident response documentation and update it regularly. Moreover, organizations should establish communication channels and escalation procedures to ensure timely notification and coordination during security incidents. CLI commands can automate the configuration of notification systems and incident response communication tools. For example, organizations can use the Twilio CLI to set up SMS alerts or use the AWS CLI to configure Amazon SNS (Simple Notification Service) topics for sending notifications to relevant stakeholders. Continuous monitoring and detection capabilities are essential for identifying security incidents as they occur in cloud environments. CLI commands can automate the deployment of monitoring agents and sensors, enabling organizations to detect and respond to security threats in real-time. For example, organizations can use the Azure CLI to deploy Azure Security Center agents on virtual machines or use AWS CLI to enable Amazon GuardDuty for threat detection and monitoring. Additionally, organizations must establish incident response playbooks that define roles and responsibilities for different members of the incident response team. CLI commands can automate the assignment of tasks and responsibilities, ensuring that each team member knows their role in responding to security incidents. For instance, organizations can use workflow automation tools like Ansible or Terraform to orchestrate incident response workflows and assign tasks based on predefined roles. Furthermore, organizations should conduct regular tabletop exercises and simulations to test the effectiveness of their incident response plans and procedures. CLI commands can facilitate the execution of tabletop exercises by automating scenario creation and simulation. For example, organizations can use Python scripts to generate simulated security incidents and use CLI commands to trigger alerts and notifications as part of the exercise. Documentation and post-incident analysis are critical aspects of developing cloud-specific incident response plans. CLI commands can automate the generation of incident reports and documentation, enabling organizations to capture lessons learned and improve their incident response capabilities over time. For instance, organizations can use the ELK Stack (Elasticsearch, Logstash, Kibana) to aggregate and analyze log data from incident response activities and generate reports using CLI commands. In conclusion, developing cloud-

specific incident response plans requires careful planning, coordination, and automation. CLI commands offer a versatile and efficient means of deploying and managing incident response procedures, enabling organizations to detect, respond to, and recover from security incidents effectively in cloud environments. By leveraging CLI commands to automate incident detection, communication, monitoring, and documentation tasks, organizations can strengthen their incident response capabilities and minimize the impact of security breaches and incidents on their cloud infrastructure and data.
Coordinating incident response across multiple cloud providers presents unique challenges that require careful planning and coordination to ensure effective incident resolution. CLI commands play a crucial role in facilitating cross-provider incident response by enabling organizations to manage and coordinate response activities seamlessly. One of the primary challenges in coordinating incident response across cloud providers is the disparate nature of cloud environments and the lack of centralized visibility into security incidents. CLI commands can help address this challenge by providing automation capabilities for collecting and aggregating security event data from multiple

cloud platforms. For example, organizations can use the Azure CLI to retrieve security event logs from Azure Security Center or use the AWS CLI to query AWS CloudTrail logs. Additionally, organizations must establish clear lines of communication and coordination with each cloud provider's incident response team to ensure timely notification and collaboration during security incidents. CLI commands can automate communication tasks by enabling organizations to set up incident notification channels and escalation procedures. For instance, organizations can use Slack CLI commands to create incident response channels and invite relevant stakeholders from each cloud provider. Moreover, organizations should develop standardized incident response procedures and playbooks that account for the unique characteristics of each cloud provider's environment. CLI commands can automate the deployment of incident response playbooks and workflows, ensuring consistency and efficiency in incident response activities. For example, organizations can use Ansible or Terraform scripts to deploy incident response playbooks across multiple cloud environments. Furthermore, organizations must conduct regular tabletop exercises and simulations to test their cross-provider incident response capabilities and identify areas for improvement. CLI commands can facilitate the execution of tabletop exercises by automating scenario creation and simulation tasks. For instance, organizations can use Python scripts to generate simulated security incidents across multiple cloud platforms and use CLI commands to trigger alerts and notifications as part of the exercise. Documentation and post-incident analysis are essential aspects of coordinating incident response across cloud providers. CLI commands can automate the generation of incident reports and documentation, enabling organizations to capture lessons learned and improve their incident response processes over time. For example, organizations can use the ELK Stack to aggregate and analyze log data from incident response activities and generate reports using CLI commands. In conclusion, coordinating incident response across multiple cloud providers requires careful planning, communication, and automation. CLI commands offer a versatile and efficient means of managing and coordinating incident response activities, enabling organizations to detect, respond to, and recover from security incidents effectively across diverse cloud environments. By leveraging CLI commands to automate communication, deployment, and documentation tasks, organizations can strengthen their cross-provider incident response capabilities and minimize the impact of security breaches and incidents on their cloud infrastructure and data.

Chapter 10: Optimization and Fine-Tuning for Cloud Security Excellence

Performance optimization strategies for security controls are essential for maintaining the effectiveness of security measures while minimizing impact on system performance. CLI commands play a crucial role in implementing these strategies by providing automation and efficiency in security control management. One key strategy for optimizing security controls is to prioritize critical security functions based on risk assessment and business impact analysis. CLI commands can automate the deployment of security controls and policies, enabling organizations to focus resources on protecting high-value assets and critical systems. For example, organizations can use the AWS CLI to prioritize security group rules and network ACLs to ensure that critical applications and services have the necessary access controls in place. Additionally, organizations should leverage caching and load balancing techniques to reduce the overhead of security inspection and enforcement. CLI commands can be used to configure caching servers and load balancers to offload repetitive security tasks and improve response times. For instance, organizations can use NGINX CLI commands to configure caching and load balancing rules for web applications, reducing the need for repeated security checks on incoming requests. Moreover, organizations should implement intelligent traffic shaping and rate limiting mechanisms to mitigate the impact of denial-of-service (DoS) attacks and other forms of malicious traffic. CLI commands can automate the deployment of traffic shaping policies and rate limiting rules, enabling organizations to protect against DoS attacks while maintaining optimal performance. For example, organizations can use iptables CLI commands on Linux-based servers to implement rate limiting rules that throttle incoming traffic from suspicious IP addresses. Furthermore, organizations should optimize encryption and decryption processes to minimize the performance impact of cryptographic operations. CLI commands can be used to configure encryption settings and key management policies, enabling organizations to strike a balance between security and performance. For example, organizations can use OpenSSL CLI commands to generate and manage SSL/TLS certificates and configure encryption algorithms and key lengths based on performance requirements. Additionally, organizations should leverage hardware acceleration technologies such as cryptographic accelerators and secure enclaves to offload cryptographic operations from the CPU and improve performance. CLI commands can automate the configuration of hardware acceleration features, enabling organizations to enhance security without sacrificing performance. For example, organizations can use the openssl engine CLI command to enable hardware-based encryption and decryption on supported cryptographic accelerators. Moreover, organizations should implement efficient logging and monitoring practices to capture relevant security events and metrics without overwhelming system resources. CLI commands can automate the deployment of logging and monitoring agents, enabling organizations to collect and analyze security data in real-time. For example, organizations can use the Azure CLI to deploy Azure Monitor agents on virtual machines to capture security-related events and performance metrics. In conclusion, performance optimization strategies for security controls are essential for maintaining effective security posture while minimizing impact on system performance. CLI commands offer a powerful toolset for implementing these strategies, enabling organizations to automate the deployment and management of security controls while maintaining optimal performance levels. By leveraging CLI commands to prioritize critical security functions, implement caching and load balancing techniques, optimize encryption processes, leverage hardware acceleration technologies, and implement efficient logging and monitoring practices, organizations can strengthen their security posture while ensuring optimal system performance. Continuous improvement in cloud security posture is vital for organizations to adapt to evolving threats and vulnerabilities in dynamic cloud environments. CLI commands play a pivotal role in this process by providing automation and efficiency in implementing security enhancements and best practices. One key aspect of continuous improvement is the regular assessment of cloud security controls and configurations to identify weaknesses and areas for enhancement. CLI commands can automate security assessments by scanning cloud resources for misconfigurations and vulnerabilities. For example, organizations can use the AWS CLI to run automated security checks using AWS Config rules or use third-party tools like CloudCheckr or Tenable.io to assess cloud security posture. Additionally, organizations should leverage threat intelligence feeds and security advisories to stay informed about emerging threats and vulnerabilities relevant to their cloud environment. CLI commands can automate the retrieval and analysis of threat intelligence data, enabling organizations to prioritize security enhancements based on real-time threat information. For instance, organizations can use the curl command to query threat intelligence APIs or use Python scripts to parse threat feeds and identify relevant security threats. Moreover, organizations should establish a robust patch management process to promptly address security vulnerabilities and software flaws in cloud infrastructure and applications. CLI commands can automate patch management tasks by deploying security patches and updates across cloud resources. For example, organizations can use the Azure CLI to apply updates to virtual machine images or use configuration management tools like Puppet or Ansible to automate patch deployment on cloud servers. Furthermore, organizations should implement proactive security measures such as intrusion detection and prevention systems (IDS/IPS) and security information and event management (SIEM) solutions to detect and respond to security incidents in real-time. CLI commands can automate the deployment and configuration of these security tools, enabling organizations to enhance their detection and response capabilities. For instance, organizations can use the GCP CLI to enable Google Cloud IDS or use the Elastic Stack CLI to deploy SIEM agents on cloud servers. Additionally, organizations should conduct regular security awareness training for employees to educate them about best practices and security policies relevant to cloud environments. CLI commands can facilitate security training by automating the deployment of training materials and resources. For example, organizations can use the SCP (Secure Copy Protocol) CLI command to transfer security training videos and documents to employee workstations or use the AWS CLI to create S3 buckets for hosting security training materials. Moreover, organizations should establish incident response playbooks and conduct regular tabletop exercises to test their incident response procedures. CLI commands can automate incident response workflows by orchestrating response activities and assigning tasks to incident response teams. For instance, organizations can use the Azure CLI to create Azure Logic Apps that automate incident response workflows or use the AWS CLI to trigger Lambda functions for automated incident remediation. In conclusion, continuous improvement in cloud security posture is essential for organizations to mitigate emerging threats and vulnerabilities effectively. CLI commands offer a versatile and efficient means of implementing security enhancements and best practices, enabling organizations to automate security assessments, patch management, threat intelligence analysis, proactive security measures, security awareness training, and incident response workflows. By leveraging CLI commands to automate these tasks, organizations can strengthen their cloud security posture and adapt to evolving security challenges in dynamic cloud environments.

BOOK 3

ADVANCED CLOUD SECURITY STRATEGIES EXPERT INSIGHTS INTO NIST COMPLIANCE AND BEYOND

ROB BOTWRIGHT

Chapter 1: Exploring NIST Compliance Framework Components

The National Institute of Standards and Technology (NIST) is a renowned agency within the United States Department of Commerce that plays a pivotal role in developing standards and guidelines to enhance the security and effectiveness of information technology and cybersecurity systems. NIST's documentation and publications serve as authoritative resources for organizations worldwide seeking to improve their cybersecurity posture and align with best practices. Understanding NIST's extensive library of documentation and publications is essential for organizations looking to implement robust cybersecurity measures and comply with industry standards and regulations. The cornerstone of NIST's cybersecurity guidance is the Special Publication (SP) series, which covers a wide range of topics spanning from risk management to cryptographic algorithms. These publications provide detailed recommendations and best practices for securing information systems and protecting sensitive data from threats and vulnerabilities. The NIST SP 800 series, in particular, is widely regarded as the gold standard for cybersecurity guidance and includes publications such as SP 800-53, SP 800-171, and SP 800-37, among others. Each SP document addresses specific aspects of cybersecurity, providing organizations with actionable recommendations and implementation guidance. For example, NIST SP 800-53 outlines security and privacy controls for federal information systems and organizations, while SP 800-171 focuses on protecting Controlled Unclassified Information (CUI) in non-federal systems and organizations. These documents are invaluable resources for organizations seeking to establish comprehensive cybersecurity programs and comply with regulatory requirements such as the Federal Information Security Modernization Act (FISMA) and the Defense Federal Acquisition Regulation Supplement (DFARS). In addition to the SP series, NIST produces other publications that cover specialized topics and emerging trends in cybersecurity. For instance, NIST Interagency Reports (NISTIRs) provide in-depth research and analysis on specific cybersecurity issues, while NIST Cybersecurity Practice Guides offer practical solutions and implementation guidance for securing IT systems and infrastructure. Furthermore, NIST Special Publications are complemented by other resources such as NIST Cybersecurity Framework (CSF), which provides a flexible framework for organizations to assess and improve their cybersecurity posture based on industry standards and best practices. The NIST CSF is widely adopted by organizations of all sizes and industries as a roadmap for managing cybersecurity risk and enhancing resilience. Moreover, NIST collaborates with industry stakeholders and government agencies to develop cybersecurity standards and guidelines that address emerging technologies and threats. For example, NIST has published guidance on securing Internet of Things (IoT) devices, cloud computing, and artificial intelligence (AI), reflecting the agency's commitment to staying at the forefront of cybersecurity innovation. To access NIST documentation and publications, organizations can visit the NIST website (nist.gov) and navigate to the Cybersecurity Publications section, where they can search and download relevant documents free of charge. Additionally, organizations can leverage CLI commands to automate the retrieval and analysis of NIST documentation, enabling them to stay up-to-date on the latest cybersecurity guidance and best practices. For example, organizations can use the curl command to download NIST publications from the agency's website or use scripting languages like Python to parse and analyze NIST documentation for specific topics or keywords. In conclusion, NIST's documentation and publications are invaluable resources for organizations seeking to enhance their cybersecurity posture and mitigate cyber risks effectively. By understanding and implementing NIST's guidance, organizations can establish robust cybersecurity programs, comply with regulatory requirements, and protect their critical assets from evolving threats in an increasingly digital world.

Understanding the NIST Risk Management Framework (RMF) is essential for organizations looking to effectively manage cybersecurity risks and protect their information systems and assets. The NIST RMF is a structured approach to managing cybersecurity risk that provides organizations with a comprehensive framework for assessing, selecting, implementing, and monitoring security controls to protect their information systems. At its core, the NIST RMF is designed to help organizations identify, assess, and prioritize risks to their information systems and develop a tailored risk management strategy to mitigate those risks effectively. The framework consists of six steps: Prepare, Categorize, Select,

Implement, Assess, and Authorize, along with continuous monitoring, which collectively provide a systematic and repeatable process for managing cybersecurity risk throughout the system development lifecycle. The first step in the NIST RMF is to Prepare, which involves establishing the context for risk management activities by defining the organization's risk management strategy, policies, and procedures. Organizations can use CLI commands to automate the preparation phase by creating documentation templates, establishing risk management roles and responsibilities, and defining risk assessment methodologies. For example, organizations can use Markdown templates and shell scripts to generate risk management documentation and assign roles and responsibilities using the AWS CLI or Azure CLI. The second step in the NIST RMF is to Categorize, which involves identifying and prioritizing information system assets and the associated risks based on their impact on the organization's mission and business objectives. CLI commands can assist organizations in categorizing information system assets by automating asset discovery and risk assessment processes. For instance, organizations can use network scanning tools like Nmap or Nessus to identify and categorize network assets or use cloud security tools like AWS Config or Azure Security Center to assess cloud-based assets automatically. The third step in the NIST RMF is to Select, which involves selecting and implementing appropriate security controls to mitigate identified risks based on the organization's risk management strategy and risk tolerance. CLI commands play a crucial role in selecting and implementing security controls by automating the deployment and configuration of security controls across information systems. For example, organizations can use configuration management tools like Ansible or Puppet to automate the deployment of security controls on cloud servers or use infrastructure-as-code tools like Terraform to define security controls as code and provision them automatically. The fourth step in the NIST RMF is to Implement, which involves implementing and configuring selected security controls in accordance with organizational policies and procedures. CLI commands can streamline the implementation phase by automating configuration tasks and ensuring consistency across information systems. For example, organizations can use scripting languages like Bash or PowerShell to automate the configuration of firewall rules, encryption settings, and access controls on network devices or use cloud management platforms like AWS CloudFormation or Azure Resource Manager to deploy standardized security configurations across cloud environments. The fifth step in the NIST RMF is to Assess, which involves assessing the effectiveness of implemented security controls in mitigating identified risks and determining compliance with organizational policies and requirements. CLI commands can facilitate the assessment phase by automating security testing and vulnerability scanning activities. For instance, organizations can use penetration testing tools like Metasploit or Burp Suite to assess the effectiveness of security controls on web applications or use vulnerability scanning tools like OpenVAS or Qualys to identify and remediate security vulnerabilities in network infrastructure. The sixth step in the NIST RMF is to Authorize, which involves reviewing the results of security control assessments and making risk-based decisions regarding the authorization of information systems for operation. CLI commands can support the authorization process by automating the generation of authorization documentation and facilitating decision-making processes. For example, organizations can use document generation tools like LaTeX or Markdown to create authorization packages and use version control systems like Git to track changes and approvals throughout the authorization process. In conclusion, understanding the NIST Risk Management Framework is essential for organizations seeking to effectively manage cybersecurity risks and protect their information systems and assets. By following the systematic and repeatable process outlined in the NIST RMF and leveraging CLI commands to automate risk management activities, organizations can develop a proactive and resilient approach to cybersecurity that enables them to adapt to evolving threats and challenges effectively.

Chapter 2: Threat Modeling Methodologies for Cloud Environments

Identifying threats and vulnerabilities in cloud infrastructure is a critical aspect of maintaining robust security posture in modern IT environments. CLI commands serve as valuable tools for identifying and addressing these security risks efficiently and effectively. One common threat in cloud infrastructure is misconfigured security settings, which can expose sensitive data to unauthorized access. CLI commands such as AWS CLI or Azure CLI allow administrators to audit cloud configurations and identify misconfigured resources. For example, using the AWS CLI, administrators can list all S3 buckets with public access permissions enabled, helping to identify potential security vulnerabilities. Another threat is insecure authentication mechanisms, which can lead to unauthorized access to cloud resources. CLI commands can assist in auditing user accounts and access controls to ensure proper authentication measures are in place. For instance, administrators can use the Google Cloud CLI to list all IAM (Identity and Access Management) policies and roles, identifying any overly permissive permissions that may pose a security risk. Additionally, vulnerabilities in cloud infrastructure can stem from outdated software or unpatched systems. CLI commands can automate vulnerability scanning and patch management processes to identify and remediate these weaknesses. For example, using scripting languages like Bash or Python, administrators can automate vulnerability scans across cloud instances and deploy patches using package management tools such as yum or apt-get. Furthermore, malicious actors may exploit misconfigurations in cloud infrastructure to launch attacks such as data breaches or denial-of-service (DoS) attacks. CLI commands can aid in detecting anomalous behavior and potential security incidents by analyzing logs and monitoring network traffic. For instance, administrators can use the AWS CLI to query CloudTrail logs or use the Elastic Stack CLI to analyze logs for suspicious activity, helping to detect and respond to security threats promptly. Additionally, vulnerabilities may arise from inadequate encryption or data protection measures, leaving sensitive information exposed to interception or theft. CLI commands can facilitate the implementation of encryption protocols and data protection mechanisms to mitigate these risks. For example, administrators can use OpenSSL CLI commands to generate and manage SSL/TLS certificates for securing network communications or use encryption tools like GPG (GNU Privacy Guard) to encrypt sensitive data before storing it in the cloud. Moreover, administrators must be vigilant against insider threats, where authorized users misuse their privileges to compromise cloud security. CLI commands can help monitor user activity and detect suspicious behavior indicative of insider threats. For example, administrators can use audit logging commands in the AWS CLI to track user actions and identify unauthorized access attempts or unusual patterns of behavior. Additionally, administrators can implement least privilege principles using CLI commands to restrict user permissions to only the resources and actions necessary for their role, reducing the potential impact of insider threats. In conclusion, identifying threats and vulnerabilities in cloud infrastructure is crucial for maintaining the security and integrity of digital assets and data. CLI commands offer a versatile and efficient means of conducting security assessments, monitoring for suspicious activity, and implementing security controls to mitigate risks effectively. By leveraging CLI commands to automate security processes and workflows, organizations can strengthen their cloud security posture and defend against evolving cyber threats.

Advanced threat modeling techniques and tools play a crucial role in identifying and mitigating cybersecurity risks in complex IT environments. CLI commands are valuable resources for implementing advanced threat modeling methodologies and enhancing the security posture of organizations. One such technique is data flow diagrams, which depict the flow of data through an application or system and help identify potential vulnerabilities and attack vectors. CLI commands can assist in creating data flow diagrams by automating the analysis of application code and network traffic. For example, administrators can use tools like Wireshark or tcpdump to capture and analyze network packets, identifying data flows and dependencies between system components. Another advanced threat modeling technique is attack surface analysis, which involves identifying all possible entry points and paths that attackers may exploit to compromise a system. CLI commands can aid in conducting attack surface analysis by automating vulnerability scanning and penetration testing activities. For instance, administrators can use tools like Nmap or Nessus to scan for open ports and services on network devices, helping to identify potential attack vectors and weaknesses in the system. Furthermore, threat modeling often involves assessing the security of third-party components and dependencies used in software development. CLI commands can streamline this process by automating the retrieval and analysis of vulnerability data from public databases and repositories. For example, administrators can use the npm CLI to check for vulnerabilities in Node.js packages or use the gem CLI to analyze Ruby gems for security issues. Additionally, threat modeling encompasses the identification and prioritization of potential threats and adversaries targeting an organization's assets and infrastructure. CLI commands can assist in this process by automating threat intelligence gathering and analysis. For instance, administrators can use tools like Shodan or Censys to search for exposed devices and services on the internet, helping to identify potential threats and assess their capabilities. Moreover, threat modeling involves evaluating the likelihood and impact of potential security incidents and breaches. CLI commands can aid in conducting risk assessments and quantifying the potential impact of threats on an organization's operations and assets. For example, administrators can use scripting languages like

Python or PowerShell to automate risk assessment calculations and generate risk heatmaps based on threat likelihood and impact severity. Additionally, threat modeling often involves simulating potential attack scenarios and assessing the effectiveness of existing security controls and countermeasures. CLI commands can facilitate this process by automating the deployment and orchestration of attack simulations and penetration testing exercises. For instance, administrators can use tools like Metasploit or OWASP ZAP to simulate common attack techniques such as SQL injection or cross-site scripting (XSS) attacks, helping to identify weaknesses in the system and validate the effectiveness of security controls. In conclusion, advanced threat modeling techniques and tools are essential components of a comprehensive cybersecurity strategy. CLI commands offer a versatile and efficient means of implementing threat modeling methodologies, automating security assessments, and enhancing the resilience of organizations against cyber threats. By leveraging CLI commands to streamline threat modeling processes, organizations can identify and mitigate security risks effectively, ensuring the protection of their valuable assets and data.

Chapter 3: Architectural Principles and Implementation of Zero Trust in the Cloud

Zero Trust Architecture (ZTA) is a cybersecurity paradigm shift that challenges traditional security models by assuming that threats may originate from both internal and external sources and must be mitigated regardless of network location or user identity. CLI commands play a pivotal role in implementing Zero Trust Architecture principles and components, enabling organizations to enhance their security posture and protect against evolving cyber threats. At the core of Zero Trust Architecture is the principle of least privilege, which restricts access permissions to only the resources and data necessary for users or systems to perform their functions. CLI commands can assist in implementing least privilege by automating user access controls and privilege management tasks. For example, administrators can use the AWS CLI to define IAM policies that grant specific permissions to individual users or groups, ensuring that access is limited to authorized individuals. Another key component of Zero Trust Architecture is microsegmentation, which involves dividing the network into smaller, isolated segments to contain lateral movement and limit the impact of potential security breaches. CLI commands can facilitate microsegmentation by automating the configuration of network access controls and firewall rules. For instance, administrators can use tools like iptables or ufw to create firewall rules that restrict traffic between different network segments, preventing unauthorized access to sensitive resources. Additionally, Zero Trust Architecture emphasizes the importance of continuous monitoring and real-time threat detection to identify and respond to security incidents promptly. CLI commands can support continuous monitoring by automating the collection and analysis of security logs and network traffic data. For example, administrators can use the Elastic Stack CLI to deploy and manage a centralized logging and monitoring platform that aggregates logs from across the network and uses machine learning algorithms to detect anomalous behavior indicative of potential security threats. Furthermore, Zero Trust Architecture advocates for the use of strong encryption and authentication mechanisms to protect data and verify the identity of users and devices accessing the network. CLI commands can assist in implementing encryption and authentication by automating the deployment and configuration of cryptographic protocols and authentication protocols. For example, administrators can use OpenSSL CLI commands to generate and manage SSL/TLS certificates for securing network communications, or use the LDAP CLI to configure LDAP authentication for user authentication. Moreover, Zero Trust Architecture emphasizes the importance of continuous validation and verification of device trustworthiness and integrity to prevent unauthorized access and data breaches. CLI commands can support device validation by automating endpoint security checks and integrity verification processes. For instance, administrators can use the Microsoft Defender ATP CLI to conduct endpoint security assessments and identify devices that are out of compliance with security policies, helping to mitigate the risk of malware infections and other security threats. In conclusion, Zero Trust Architecture represents a paradigm shift in cybersecurity that prioritizes security over trust and assumes that threats may originate from both internal and external sources. CLI commands offer a versatile and efficient means of implementing Zero Trust Architecture principles and components, enabling organizations to strengthen their security posture and protect against evolving cyber threats effectively. By leveraging CLI commands to automate access controls, microsegmentation, continuous monitoring, encryption, authentication, and device validation, organizations can build a resilient and adaptive security infrastructure that mitigates the risk of data breaches and unauthorized access. Practical strategies for implementing Zero Trust in cloud environments are essential for organizations seeking to enhance their security posture and protect against evolving cyber threats. CLI commands play a crucial role in deploying Zero Trust principles and techniques, providing organizations with the tools needed to secure their cloud infrastructure effectively. One practical strategy for implementing Zero Trust in cloud environments is to start by defining clear security policies and access controls that adhere to the principles of least privilege and need-to-know. CLI commands can assist in defining these policies by automating the configuration of Identity and Access Management (IAM) rules and permissions. For example, administrators can use the AWS CLI to create IAM policies that restrict access to specific resources based on user roles or attributes, ensuring that only authorized individuals can access sensitive data or services. Another practical strategy is to leverage encryption and cryptographic protocols to protect data in transit and at rest within the cloud environment. CLI commands can facilitate the deployment of encryption by automating the generation and management of SSL/TLS certificates and encryption keys. For instance, administrators can use OpenSSL CLI commands to create SSL certificates for encrypting network communications between cloud services or use the AWS Key Management Service (KMS) CLI to generate and manage encryption keys for securing data stored in cloud storage services like Amazon S3. Additionally, organizations can implement network segmentation and microsegmentation techniques to limit the lateral movement of attackers within the cloud environment. CLI commands can streamline the deployment of network segmentation by automating the configuration of firewall rules and access control lists (ACLs). For example, administrators can use firewall management tools like iptables or ufw to create rules that restrict traffic between different subnets or use cloud security group CLI commands to define network access controls for virtual machines and containers deployed in the cloud. Furthermore, organizations can enhance their security posture by implementing continuous monitoring and real-time threat detection capabilities in the cloud environment. CLI commands can support continuous monitoring by automating the collection and analysis of security logs and telemetry data. For instance, administrators can use log management tools like ELK (Elasticsearch, Logstash, and Kibana) or Splunk CLI commands to aggregate and analyze logs from cloud services and infrastructure components, enabling them to detect and respond to security incidents promptly. Moreover, organizations can strengthen their Zero Trust implementation by adopting a zero-trust mindset and culture throughout the organization. CLI commands can help enforce this culture by automating security assessments and compliance checks across the cloud environment. For example, administrators can use scripting languages like Python or PowerShell to develop custom scripts that perform security audits and validate compliance with organizational policies and industry regulations. Additionally, organizations can leverage cloud-native security services and solutions to augment their Zero Trust implementation. CLI commands can facilitate the deployment of these services by automating the provisioning and configuration of security controls and monitoring tools. For instance, administrators can use cloud provider CLI commands to deploy managed security services like AWS GuardDuty or Azure Security Center, which offer built-in threat detection and remediation capabilities for cloud environments. In conclusion, practical strategies for implementing Zero Trust in cloud environments are essential for organizations looking to strengthen their security posture and protect against cyber threats. CLI commands provide organizations with the automation and control needed to deploy Zero Trust principles effectively, from defining security policies and access controls to deploying encryption and segmentation techniques. By leveraging CLI commands to automate security tasks and enforce a zero-trust mindset throughout the organization, organizations can build a resilient and adaptive security infrastructure that mitigates the risk of data breaches and unauthorized access in the cloud.

Chapter 4: Cutting-Edge Encryption Technologies for Securing Cloud Data

Homomorphic encryption represents a groundbreaking advancement in cryptography, enabling computations to be performed on encrypted data without the need to decrypt it first, thus preserving privacy and confidentiality. CLI commands can facilitate the deployment of homomorphic encryption techniques in cloud environments by automating the generation and management of cryptographic keys and configurations. For example, administrators can use the OpenSSL CLI to generate homomorphic encryption keys for securing sensitive data stored in cloud databases or use the Microsoft SEAL CLI to configure homomorphic encryption parameters for performing computations on encrypted data. One of the key applications of homomorphic encryption in the cloud is secure data processing and computation, where computations are performed directly on encrypted data without exposing the plaintext to the cloud provider or any other unauthorized parties. CLI commands can assist in deploying secure computation solutions by automating the encryption and decryption of data and managing access controls and permissions. For instance, administrators can use the PySEAL CLI to perform secure computations on encrypted data stored in cloud storage services like Google Cloud Storage or use the Microsoft SEAL CLI to encrypt and process data in real-time using homomorphic encryption techniques. Another application of homomorphic encryption in the cloud is secure data sharing and collaboration, where multiple parties can perform computations on encrypted data without revealing sensitive information to each other. CLI commands can support secure data sharing by automating the encryption and decryption of data and managing access controls and permissions. For example, administrators can use the Microsoft SEAL CLI to encrypt data before sharing it with collaborators or use the PySEAL CLI to perform computations on encrypted data received from other parties without decrypting it first. Moreover, homomorphic encryption can also be used for privacy-preserving machine learning, where computations are performed on encrypted data to train and evaluate machine learning models without exposing sensitive information to the cloud provider or any other unauthorized parties. CLI commands can assist in deploying privacy-preserving machine learning solutions by automating the encryption and decryption of data and managing access controls and permissions. For instance, administrators can use the PySEAL CLI to encrypt training data before uploading it to cloud machine learning platforms like Google Cloud AI Platform or use the Microsoft SEAL CLI to evaluate machine learning models on encrypted data without decrypting it first. Additionally, homomorphic encryption can enable secure and privacy-preserving data analytics in the cloud, where computations are performed on encrypted data to extract insights and patterns without exposing sensitive information to the cloud provider or any other unauthorized parties. CLI commands can support secure data analytics by automating the encryption and decryption of data and managing access controls and permissions. For example, administrators can use the Microsoft SEAL CLI to perform data analytics on encrypted data stored in cloud data warehouses like Amazon Redshift or use the PySEAL CLI to run queries on encrypted data in real-time without decrypting it first. In conclusion, homomorphic encryption offers a powerful solution for preserving privacy and confidentiality in cloud environments, enabling secure data processing, sharing, machine learning, and analytics without compromising sensitive information. CLI commands provide organizations with the automation and control needed to deploy homomorphic encryption techniques effectively, ensuring the protection of data and privacy in the cloud. Post-Quantum Cryptography (PQC) represents a significant advancement in the field of cryptography, aimed at ensuring the long-term security of data in the face of quantum computing threats. CLI commands are instrumental in deploying post-quantum cryptographic algorithms and protocols, providing organizations with the tools needed to future-proof their cloud data protection strategies. One of the primary motivations for adopting post-quantum cryptography is the potential threat posed by quantum computers to traditional cryptographic systems, which rely on the difficulty of certain mathematical problems for their security. CLI commands can assist in deploying post-quantum cryptographic algorithms by automating the generation and management of cryptographic keys and configurations. For example, administrators can use the OpenSSL CLI to generate post-quantum cryptographic keys for securing sensitive data stored in cloud databases or use the Microsoft PQCrypto CLI to configure post-quantum cryptographic parameters for encrypting and decrypting data in transit. Post-quantum cryptography offers several advantages over traditional cryptographic systems, including resistance to attacks from quantum computers and enhanced security guarantees against various cryptographic vulnerabilities. CLI commands play a crucial role in deploying post-quantum cryptographic algorithms and protocols, providing organizations with the automation and control needed to secure their cloud data effectively. For instance, administrators can use the pqRSA CLI to encrypt and decrypt data using post-quantum cryptographic algorithms like lattice-based cryptography or use the pqCrypto CLI to sign and verify messages using post-quantum cryptographic signatures. Another advantage of post-quantum cryptography is its compatibility with existing cryptographic standards and protocols, allowing organizations to integrate post-quantum cryptographic algorithms seamlessly into their existing security infrastructure. CLI commands can facilitate the integration of post-quantum cryptography by automating the configuration of cryptographic parameters and protocols. For example, administrators can use the pqTLS CLI to configure Transport Layer Security (TLS) connections using post-quantum cryptographic algorithms like hash-based cryptography or use the pqSSH CLI to establish Secure Shell (SSH) connections using post-quantum cryptographic key exchange mechanisms. Moreover, post-quantum cryptography offers the promise of long-term security and resilience against future advances in quantum computing technology, ensuring that data protected with post-quantum cryptographic algorithms remains secure even as quantum computers become more powerful. CLI commands can support long-term security by automating the deployment and management of post-quantum cryptographic algorithms and protocols. For instance, administrators can use the pqCrypto CLI to rotate cryptographic keys periodically or use the pqSecurity CLI to monitor and audit the usage of post-quantum cryptographic algorithms in the cloud environment. In conclusion, post-quantum cryptography represents a crucial step forward in securing cloud data against the threat of quantum computing, offering long-term security and resilience against future cryptographic attacks. CLI commands provide organizations with the automation and control needed to deploy post-quantum cryptographic algorithms and protocols effectively, ensuring the protection of sensitive data in the cloud for years to come.

Chapter 5: Container Security: Challenges and Solutions

Containerization technologies have revolutionized the way software applications are developed, deployed, and managed in modern computing environments. CLI commands play a crucial role in working with containerization technologies, providing developers and administrators with the tools needed to create, run, and manage containers effectively. One of the most popular containerization technologies is Docker, which allows developers to package their applications and dependencies into lightweight, portable containers that can run consistently across different environments. CLI commands such as docker build, docker run, and docker-compose enable developers to build, deploy, and manage Docker containers with ease. Another widely used containerization technology is Kubernetes, an open-source container orchestration platform that automates the deployment, scaling, and management of containerized applications. CLI commands like kubectl allow administrators to interact with Kubernetes clusters, deploy applications, and manage resources such as pods, services, and deployments. Containerization technologies offer numerous benefits, including increased efficiency, portability, and scalability. CLI commands provide developers and administrators with the flexibility to automate various tasks related to container management, improving productivity and reducing manual effort. Additionally, containerization technologies facilitate microservices architectures, where applications are decomposed into smaller, loosely coupled services that can be developed, deployed, and scaled independently. CLI commands empower developers to create and manage microservices-based applications efficiently, enabling them to focus on building features and delivering value to end-users. Furthermore, containerization technologies enhance security by isolating applications and their dependencies within individual containers, reducing the risk of software conflicts and vulnerabilities. CLI commands enable administrators to enforce security policies, monitor container activity, and respond to security incidents proactively. Moreover, containerization technologies streamline the process of continuous integration and continuous delivery (CI/CD), allowing organizations to automate the building, testing, and deployment of software applications. CLI commands such as docker-compose and kubectl enable developers to define and orchestrate complex deployment pipelines, ensuring consistent and reliable delivery of applications. Additionally, containerization technologies facilitate hybrid and multi-cloud deployments, where applications can be deployed across on-premises infrastructure and public cloud platforms seamlessly. CLI commands empower administrators to manage containerized workloads across different environments, providing flexibility and agility in deploying and scaling applications. In conclusion, containerization technologies have transformed the way software applications are developed, deployed, and managed, offering numerous benefits in terms of efficiency, scalability, and security. CLI commands play a vital role in working with containerization technologies, providing developers and administrators with the automation and control needed to leverage the full potential of containers in modern computing environments.

Container security is paramount in ensuring the integrity and protection of applications and data running within containers in modern computing environments. CLI commands play a crucial role in implementing best practices for container security and mitigating risks effectively. One fundamental best practice for container security is to use trusted base images from reputable sources when building containers, as insecure or outdated base images can introduce vulnerabilities into the containerized environment. CLI commands such as docker pull enable developers to pull base images from trusted repositories like Docker Hub or private registries hosted within the organization. Additionally, it is essential to regularly update and patch container images to address known vulnerabilities and mitigate security risks. CLI commands such as docker image update facilitate the process of updating container images with the latest security patches and fixes. Furthermore, implementing least privilege access controls is critical for minimizing the attack surface and limiting the capabilities of containers to only what is necessary for their intended functionality. CLI commands like docker run --cap-drop=<capability> allow administrators to restrict the capabilities available to containers, reducing the risk of privilege escalation attacks. Another best practice for container security is to enforce network segmentation and isolation to prevent unauthorized access to sensitive resources and data within the containerized environment. CLI commands such as docker network create enable administrators to create isolated network segments for containers, ensuring that communication between containers is restricted to only what is necessary for their operation. Moreover, enabling container runtime security features such as seccomp and AppArmor can provide an additional layer of defense against malicious attacks and exploits targeting the container runtime environment. CLI commands like docker run --security-opt=<option> allow administrators to configure runtime security options for containers, enhancing their resilience against security threats. Additionally, implementing container image scanning and vulnerability management tools can help identify and remediate security vulnerabilities in container images before they are deployed into production environments. CLI commands such as trivy image <image_name> enable administrators to scan container images for known vulnerabilities and prioritize remediation efforts accordingly. Furthermore, implementing runtime monitoring and logging solutions can provide visibility into container activity and help detect and respond to security incidents in real-time. CLI commands like docker stats and docker logs enable administrators to monitor container resource usage and access container logs for troubleshooting and security analysis purposes. Additionally, securing the container orchestration platform, such as Kubernetes, is crucial for ensuring the overall security of containerized workloads and infrastructure. CLI commands like kubectl apply -f <manifest_file> enable administrators to deploy security policies and configurations to Kubernetes clusters, enforcing security best practices and mitigating risks. Moreover, educating developers and administrators about container security best practices and providing training on secure coding practices and threat modeling can help foster a security-aware culture within the organization. CLI commands such as docker security <command> provide access to security-related documentation and resources, helping teams stay informed about the latest security trends and best practices. In conclusion, implementing best practices for container security and mitigating risks is essential for ensuring the integrity and protection of containerized applications and data. CLI commands play a vital role in implementing security controls, monitoring container activity, and responding to security incidents effectively, helping organizations build secure and resilient containerized environments.

Chapter 6: Securing Serverless Architectures: Strategies and Considerations

Serverless computing represents a paradigm shift in the way applications are developed, deployed, and managed in cloud environments, offering a server-centric approach where developers can focus solely on writing code without having to manage underlying infrastructure. CLI commands play a vital role in working with serverless computing platforms, providing developers and administrators with the tools needed to deploy, configure, and manage serverless applications effectively. One of the key concepts of serverless computing is the idea of functions as a service (FaaS), where developers can write individual functions that are triggered by events and executed in response to those events. CLI commands such as aws lambda create-function enable developers to create and deploy serverless functions to platforms like AWS Lambda, Azure Functions, or Google Cloud Functions. Another aspect of serverless computing is its event-driven nature, where functions are invoked in response to various events such as HTTP requests, database changes, or file uploads. CLI commands like aws lambda invoke allow developers to trigger serverless functions manually or simulate event sources for testing purposes. Additionally, serverless computing platforms offer auto-scaling capabilities, allowing functions to automatically scale up or down based on demand without requiring manual intervention from developers or administrators. CLI commands such as aws lambda update-function-configuration enable developers to configure auto-scaling policies and thresholds for serverless functions, ensuring optimal performance and cost-efficiency. Furthermore, serverless computing platforms abstract away the complexities of infrastructure management, allowing developers to focus on writing code and delivering business value. CLI commands like aws lambda deploy enable developers to deploy entire serverless applications, including functions, event sources, and dependencies, with a single command, streamlining the deployment process. Moreover, serverless computing offers cost benefits by charging users only for the resources consumed by their functions, eliminating the need to provision and pay for idle infrastructure. CLI commands such as aws lambda list-functions enable administrators to monitor usage and track costs associated with serverless functions, helping optimize resource allocation and budgeting. Additionally, serverless computing platforms provide built-in scalability, reliability, and fault tolerance, leveraging cloud provider infrastructure to ensure high availability and resilience of serverless applications. CLI commands like aws lambda list-events enable administrators to view and manage event sources that trigger serverless functions, ensuring seamless integration with external services and systems. Another advantage of serverless computing is its support for microservices architectures, where applications are decomposed into smaller, loosely coupled services that can be independently developed, deployed, and scaled. CLI commands such as aws lambda list-layers enable developers to manage shared libraries and dependencies used by serverless functions, facilitating code reuse and modularity. Furthermore, serverless computing platforms offer integrations with various cloud services and third-party APIs, enabling developers to build serverless applications that leverage a wide range of functionalities and capabilities. CLI commands like aws lambda list-aliases enable developers to manage aliases and versions of serverless functions, providing flexibility and control over deployment and rollback strategies. In conclusion, understanding the serverless computing paradigm is essential for developers and administrators looking to leverage its benefits in building scalable, cost-effective, and resilient cloud applications. CLI commands play a critical role in working with serverless computing platforms, providing the automation and control needed to deploy, manage, and monitor serverless applications effectively.

Security best practices are paramount for ensuring the integrity, confidentiality, and availability of serverless applications deployed in cloud environments. CLI commands play a crucial role in implementing these best practices and ensuring that serverless applications are protected against various security threats and vulnerabilities. One fundamental aspect of securing serverless applications is implementing proper authentication and authorization mechanisms to control access to resources and functions. CLI commands such as aws iam create-role enable administrators to create IAM roles with specific permissions for accessing resources and invoking functions within serverless applications. Additionally, using AWS Identity and Access Management (IAM) policies, administrators can define fine-grained access controls to restrict privileges and enforce the principle of least privilege. CLI commands like aws iam put-role-policy allow administrators to attach IAM policies to roles, specifying the actions and resources that users or roles are allowed to access. Furthermore, securing serverless applications requires implementing encryption mechanisms to protect sensitive data both in transit and at rest. CLI commands such as aws kms create-key enable administrators to create encryption keys using AWS Key Management Service (KMS), which can be used to encrypt data within serverless applications. Additionally, AWS Lambda functions can be configured to encrypt data using client-side encryption libraries or AWS SDKs, ensuring that data is encrypted before being stored or transmitted. Another critical aspect of serverless application security is securing the underlying infrastructure and runtime environment. CLI commands such as aws lambda update-function-configuration enable administrators to configure security settings for Lambda functions, including setting resource-based policies, configuring VPC settings, and enabling network access controls. Moreover, implementing runtime security controls such as AWS Lambda environment variables, AWS Secrets Manager, and AWS Systems Manager Parameter Store can help protect sensitive information such as API keys, database credentials, and configuration settings. CLI commands like aws lambda update-function-configuration enable administrators to manage environment variables and secrets for Lambda functions securely. Additionally, serverless applications should be designed with security in mind, following best practices for secure coding, input validation, and output encoding to prevent common security vulnerabilities such as injection attacks, cross-site scripting (XSS), and cross-site request forgery (CSRF). CLI commands such as aws lambda update-function-code enable developers to update and deploy code changes to Lambda functions securely, ensuring that security fixes and patches are applied promptly. Furthermore, implementing continuous security testing and monitoring practices is essential for identifying and mitigating security risks in serverless applications. CLI commands such as aws lambda publish-version enable developers to create and publish new versions of Lambda functions, allowing them to track changes and rollback to previous versions if necessary. Moreover, integrating security testing tools such as AWS Security Hub, AWS Config, and AWS CloudTrail into the CI/CD pipeline can help automate security checks and provide visibility into security events and incidents. CLI commands like aws securityhub enable administrators to enable and configure AWS Security Hub, a comprehensive security service that provides centralized visibility into security findings and compliance status across AWS accounts. Additionally, implementing logging and auditing mechanisms using AWS CloudWatch Logs and AWS CloudTrail can help track and analyze user activity, function invocations, and resource access within serverless applications. CLI commands such as aws cloudtrail create-trail enable administrators to create and configure CloudTrail trails, which capture API calls and log data events for monitoring and auditing purposes. In conclusion, implementing security best practices for serverless applications is essential for protecting against various security threats and vulnerabilities in cloud environments. CLI commands play a critical role in configuring security settings, managing access controls, and monitoring security events within serverless applications, helping organizations build secure and resilient cloud-native solutions.

Chapter 7: Advanced Cloud Access Controls and Privileged Access Management

Role-Based Access Control (RBAC) is a fundamental security model used in cloud environments to manage access to resources based on roles and permissions assigned to users or groups. CLI commands play a crucial role in implementing RBAC policies and managing access controls effectively within cloud environments. One of the key concepts of RBAC is the notion of roles, which define sets of permissions that dictate what actions users can perform on resources. CLI commands such as aws iam create-role enable administrators to create custom IAM roles with specific permissions tailored to the needs of different users or groups. Additionally, AWS Identity and Access Management (IAM) provides predefined AWS managed policies that define common sets of permissions for various AWS services, simplifying the process of configuring access controls. CLI commands like aws iam attach-role-policy allow administrators to attach managed policies to IAM roles, granting users or groups the necessary permissions to perform specific actions within the AWS environment. Moreover, RBAC allows administrators to assign roles to users or groups based on their responsibilities and job functions, ensuring that users have the appropriate level of access required to perform their tasks. CLI commands such as aws iam add-user-to-group enable administrators to add users to IAM groups, which can then be associated with roles containing the necessary permissions. Furthermore, RBAC supports the principle of least privilege, which dictates that users should only be granted the minimum level of access required to perform their job functions. CLI commands like aws iam put-role-policy enable administrators to define granular permissions for IAM roles, restricting access to only the resources and actions necessary for users to fulfill their duties. Additionally, RBAC enables organizations to enforce separation of duties by dividing responsibilities among different roles and ensuring that no single user has excessive privileges that could lead to security risks or compliance violations. CLI commands such as aws iam create-policy enable administrators to define custom IAM policies that enforce separation of duties and least privilege principles, enhancing security posture within the cloud environment. Moreover, RBAC facilitates centralized access control management, allowing administrators to easily review and modify access permissions across multiple users and resources from a single interface. CLI commands like aws iam list-attached-role-policies provide administrators with visibility into the policies attached to IAM roles, facilitating auditing and compliance efforts. Additionally, RBAC supports the concept of role inheritance, where users inherit permissions from roles assigned to them directly or through group membership. CLI commands like aws iam create-group enable administrators to create IAM groups, which can then be associated with roles containing the necessary permissions, enabling role inheritance for group members. Furthermore, RBAC integrates with identity federation services such as AWS Single Sign-On (SSO), enabling organizations to manage access to cloud resources centrally and enforce authentication and authorization policies consistently across hybrid environments. CLI commands like aws sso-admin create-instance-access-control-attribute-configuration enable administrators to configure instance access control attributes for AWS SSO, defining role-based access policies for federated users. In conclusion, Role-Based Access Control (RBAC) is a powerful security model that provides granular control over access to resources within cloud environments. CLI commands play a critical role in implementing RBAC policies, managing access controls, and enforcing security best practices, helping organizations achieve compliance and protect against unauthorized access and data breaches in the cloud. Privileged Access Management (PAM) strategies are essential for ensuring the security of cloud systems by controlling and monitoring access to privileged accounts and sensitive resources. CLI commands play a crucial role in implementing PAM strategies and enforcing security controls within cloud environments. One key aspect of PAM is the identification and management of privileged accounts, which have elevated permissions and access to critical resources. CLI commands such as aws iam create-user enable administrators to create IAM users, while aws iam create-group allows the creation of IAM groups for organizing users with similar roles and permissions. Additionally, administrators can assign IAM policies to users and groups using commands like aws iam attach-user-policy and aws iam attach-group-policy to grant specific permissions. Another important aspect of PAM is the enforcement of least privilege principles, which dictate that users should only be granted the minimum level of access required to perform their job functions. CLI commands such as aws iam create-policy enable administrators to define custom IAM policies with granular permissions, while aws iam put-user-policy and aws iam put-group-policy allow the attachment of policies to individual users or groups. Furthermore, implementing strong authentication mechanisms is critical for securing privileged access to cloud systems. CLI commands such as aws iam create-login-profile enable administrators to set up password-based authentication for IAM users, while aws iam create-access-key allows the creation of access keys for programmatic access. Additionally, administrators can enable multi-factor authentication (MFA) using aws iam enable-mfa-device to add an extra layer of security for accessing sensitive resources. Moreover, PAM strategies involve monitoring and auditing privileged access to detect and respond to suspicious activities or policy violations. CLI commands such as aws cloudtrail create-trail enable administrators to set up AWS CloudTrail to capture API activity logs, while aws cloudtrail start-logging initiates logging for the trail. Furthermore, administrators can configure CloudTrail to deliver logs to Amazon S3 buckets for storage and analysis using commands like aws cloudtrail update-trail. Additionally, implementing real-time monitoring solutions such as AWS CloudWatch Events and AWS Config Rules allows administrators to detect and respond to security incidents promptly. CLI commands like aws events put-rule enable administrators to create CloudWatch Events rules for monitoring specific API actions, while aws config put-config-rule allows the creation of Config rules for evaluating resource configurations against desired baselines. Moreover, privileged access should be periodically reviewed and revoked when no longer needed to reduce the risk of unauthorized access. CLI commands such as aws iam list-users and aws iam list-groups provide administrators with visibility into existing IAM users and groups, while aws iam list-attached-user-policies and aws iam list-attached-group-policies allow administrators to view attached policies. Furthermore, administrators can use commands like aws iam remove-user-from-group and aws iam delete-user to remove users from groups or delete users altogether. Additionally, implementing Just-In-Time (JIT) privilege elevation mechanisms allows administrators to grant temporary elevated access only when needed. CLI commands such as aws ssm start-session enable administrators to start a session manager session for accessing EC2 instances without exposing SSH/RDP ports.

Moreover, administrators can leverage AWS Systems Manager Parameter Store and AWS Secrets Manager to securely store and manage privileged credentials, reducing the risk of credential exposure. CLI commands like aws ssm put-parameter enable administrators to store sensitive data in Parameter Store, while aws secretsmanager create-secret allows the creation of secrets in Secrets Manager. In conclusion, Privileged Access Management (PAM) strategies are essential for securing cloud systems and protecting sensitive resources from unauthorized access and misuse. CLI commands provide administrators with the tools needed to implement PAM controls effectively, enforce security policies, and monitor privileged access activities within cloud environments.

Chapter 8: Leveraging Artificial Intelligence for Enhanced Cloud Security

AI-driven threat detection and response has emerged as a critical component of cloud security, leveraging artificial intelligence (AI) and machine learning (ML) algorithms to identify and mitigate security threats in real-time. CLI commands play a significant role in deploying and managing AI-driven threat detection and response systems within cloud environments. One of the key aspects of AI-driven threat detection is the use of machine learning models to analyze vast amounts of data and identify patterns indicative of malicious activity. CLI commands such as aws sagemaker create-endpoint enable administrators to deploy machine learning models as endpoints for real-time inference, while aws sagemaker create-training-job allows the training of models using labeled datasets. Additionally, administrators can use commands like aws cloudwatch put-metric-alarm to set up CloudWatch alarms for monitoring model performance and detecting anomalies. Moreover, AI-driven threat detection systems often leverage anomaly detection techniques to identify deviations from normal behavior that may indicate a security threat. CLI commands such as aws anomalydetector detect-anomaly enable administrators to utilize Amazon Lookout for Metrics to detect anomalies in time-series data, while aws cloudwatch get-metric-data retrieves metric data for analysis. Furthermore, administrators can set up CloudWatch Events rules using commands like aws events put-rule to trigger automated responses when anomalies are detected, such as sending notifications or initiating remediation actions. Additionally, AI-driven threat detection systems can analyze network traffic and logs to detect suspicious activities and potential security breaches. CLI commands like aws vpc create-flow-log enable administrators to create VPC flow logs to capture network traffic metadata, while aws logs put-log-events allows the ingestion of log data into CloudWatch Logs for analysis. Moreover, administrators can deploy intrusion detection and prevention systems (IDPS) using commands such as aws waf create-web-acl to set up AWS WAF web access control lists for filtering and monitoring HTTP traffic. Furthermore, AI-driven threat detection systems can integrate with security information and event management (SIEM) platforms to correlate and analyze security events across the cloud environment. CLI commands like aws securityhub enable-security-hub enable administrators to enable AWS Security Hub for aggregating and prioritizing security findings from multiple AWS services, while aws guardduty enable-guard-duty activates Amazon GuardDuty for continuous threat detection. Additionally, administrators can configure AWS Lambda functions using commands such as aws lambda create-function to automate responses to security events detected by AI-driven threat detection systems. Moreover, AI-driven threat detection systems can leverage threat intelligence feeds and indicators of compromise (IOCs) to enhance detection capabilities. CLI commands like aws securityhub import-findings enable administrators to import security findings from external sources into AWS Security Hub for correlation and analysis, while aws guardduty create-detector creates a new detector in Amazon GuardDuty for monitoring account activity and identifying potential threats. Furthermore, administrators can deploy security orchestration, automation, and response (SOAR) platforms using commands such as aws ssm create-automation to automate incident response workflows and streamline remediation efforts. Additionally, AI-driven threat detection systems can benefit from continuous training and refinement of machine learning models to adapt to evolving threats. CLI commands like aws sagemaker update-endpoint enable administrators to update deployed machine learning models with new training data and retrain them periodically to improve accuracy and effectiveness. In conclusion, AI-driven threat detection and response is a powerful approach to enhancing cloud security, leveraging artificial intelligence and machine learning techniques to detect and mitigate security threats in real-time. CLI commands provide administrators with the tools needed to deploy, manage, and integrate AI-driven threat detection systems within cloud environments, enabling proactive threat detection and effective incident response capabilities. Machine learning applications have become increasingly prevalent in anomaly detection within cloud environments, offering advanced capabilities to identify unusual patterns or behaviors that may indicate security threats or system abnormalities. CLI commands play a vital role in deploying and managing machine learning models for anomaly detection in the cloud. One of the key applications of machine learning in anomaly detection is the use of unsupervised learning algorithms to analyze data and identify patterns that deviate from normal behavior. CLI commands such as aws sagemaker create-model enable administrators to deploy machine learning models on Amazon SageMaker, while aws sagemaker create-endpoint allows for the creation of endpoints to serve real-time predictions based on incoming data. Additionally, administrators can use commands like aws sagemaker create-training-job to train machine learning models using historical datasets. Furthermore, anomaly detection models often rely on feature engineering to extract relevant information from raw data and improve the accuracy of anomaly detection algorithms. CLI commands such as aws sagemaker feature-store create-feature-group enable administrators to create feature groups in Amazon SageMaker Feature Store for storing and managing features, while aws sagemaker create-transform-job allows for data preprocessing tasks such as feature scaling or normalization. Moreover, administrators can use techniques like autoencoders or clustering algorithms to detect anomalies in high-dimensional data, such as network traffic or system logs. CLI commands like aws sagemaker create-processing-job enable administrators to preprocess data before training or inference, while aws sagemaker create-transform-job allows for batch inference on large datasets. Additionally, administrators can leverage Amazon CloudWatch Logs Insights using commands such as aws logs create-log-group to ingest and analyze log data for anomaly detection purposes. Furthermore, machine learning models for anomaly detection often require continuous monitoring and retraining to adapt to evolving patterns and maintain effectiveness over time. CLI commands such as aws cloudwatch put-metric-alarm enable administrators to set up CloudWatch alarms to monitor model performance metrics, while aws sagemaker create-model and aws sagemaker update-model allow for the deployment and updating of machine learning models with new training data. Moreover, administrators can use commands like aws cloudwatch put-metric-data to publish custom metrics to CloudWatch for monitoring purposes. Additionally, anomaly detection systems can benefit from ensemble learning techniques, which combine multiple models to improve detection accuracy and robustness. CLI commands such as aws sagemaker create-model enable administrators to deploy multiple models as endpoints, while aws sagemaker create-endpoint-configuration allows for the creation of endpoint configurations to route traffic to different models based on predefined rules. Furthermore, administrators can use techniques like model stacking or voting classifiers to combine predictions from multiple models and make final decisions. Moreover, anomaly detection models can be deployed at various layers of the cloud infrastructure, including network traffic analysis, system logs, and application behavior monitoring. CLI commands like aws sagemaker create-endpoint enable administrators to deploy machine learning models as endpoints for real-time inference, while aws ec2 create-flow-logs allows for the creation of VPC flow logs to capture network traffic metadata. Additionally, administrators can use commands such as aws logs put-log-events to ingest log data into CloudWatch Logs for analysis. Furthermore, administrators can deploy anomaly detection models using serverless computing platforms like AWS Lambda, enabling cost-effective and scalable deployment options. CLI commands such as aws lambda create-function enable administrators to create Lambda functions for processing incoming data and making real-time predictions, while aws lambda invoke allows for testing the function's behavior before deployment. Additionally, administrators can use AWS Step Functions with Lambda to orchestrate complex workflows for anomaly detection and response. In conclusion, machine learning applications for anomaly detection offer powerful capabilities to enhance security and performance monitoring in cloud environments. CLI commands provide administrators with the tools needed to deploy, manage, and integrate machine learning models effectively, enabling proactive anomaly detection and efficient incident response capabilities.

Chapter 9: Forensic Investigation Techniques in Cloud Incidents

Cloud-specific forensic challenges present unique considerations for digital investigators and cybersecurity professionals tasked with investigating incidents and breaches within cloud environments. CLI commands are instrumental in addressing these challenges and facilitating forensic investigations in the cloud. One significant challenge in cloud forensics is the dynamic and distributed nature of cloud infrastructure, which can complicate evidence collection and preservation. CLI commands such as aws s3 cp enable investigators to copy data from Amazon S3 buckets to secure storage for analysis, while aws ec2 create-image allows for the creation of Amazon Machine Images (AMIs) for capturing the state of EC2 instances at a specific point in time. Additionally, investigators can leverage AWS CloudTrail to audit API activity and track changes to cloud resources using commands like aws cloudtrail lookup-events to search for specific API calls related to the incident. Another challenge is the multi-tenant nature of cloud environments, where multiple customers share physical infrastructure, potentially leading to cross-contamination of evidence. CLI commands like aws ec2 describe-instances enable investigators to gather information about EC2 instances, including metadata and associated security groups, while aws rds describe-db-instances provides details about RDS database instances. Moreover, investigators can use AWS Organizations to enforce segregation between accounts and isolate resources using commands such as aws organizations create-account to create separate AWS accounts for each tenant. Furthermore, the vast amount of data generated in cloud environments can overwhelm traditional forensic tools and processes, necessitating the use of scalable and automated solutions. CLI commands such as aws s3api list-objects allow investigators to enumerate objects within an S3 bucket, while aws athena start-query-execution enables querying data stored in Amazon Athena for forensic analysis. Additionally, investigators can deploy AWS Lambda functions with commands like aws lambda create-function to automate repetitive tasks such as log analysis and anomaly detection. Another consideration is the ephemeral nature of cloud resources, where data and metadata may be automatically deleted or overwritten, potentially compromising forensic evidence. CLI commands like aws cloudwatchlogs create-log-group enable investigators to create log groups in CloudWatch Logs for storing application and system logs, while aws s3api put-object allows for the uploading of forensic artifacts to Amazon S3 for preservation. Moreover, investigators can use AWS Config with commands such as aws config start-configuration-recorder to record changes to cloud resources and maintain an audit trail of configuration changes over time. Additionally, the global nature of cloud infrastructure introduces jurisdictional challenges and legal complexities, requiring investigators to navigate international laws and regulations. CLI commands like aws organizations create-organization enable organizations to establish a global governance structure, while aws kms create-key allows for the creation of AWS KMS keys for encrypting sensitive data at rest and in transit. Furthermore, investigators can use AWS Artifact to access compliance reports and certifications required for legal proceedings using commands such as aws artifact get-assessment-report. Moreover, collaboration and coordination between multiple stakeholders, including cloud service providers, legal teams, and law enforcement agencies, are essential for effective cloud forensics investigations. CLI commands such as aws organizations invite-account-to-organization enable organizations to invite external parties to collaborate within an AWS Organization, while aws securityhub invite-members allows for the invitation of other AWS accounts to participate in security assessments through AWS Security Hub. Additionally, investigators can use AWS Systems Manager with commands like aws ssm start-automation-execution to automate incident response workflows and streamline communication between response teams. In conclusion, addressing cloud-specific forensic challenges requires a combination of technical expertise, effective tools, and collaboration among stakeholders. CLI commands provide investigators with the capabilities needed to collect, preserve, and analyze digital evidence in cloud environments, enabling thorough and effective forensic investigations.

Incident response and forensic investigation best practices are critical components of cybersecurity strategy, ensuring organizations can effectively detect, contain, and mitigate security incidents to minimize their impact. CLI commands play a crucial role in implementing these best practices and facilitating timely and thorough incident response efforts. One key aspect of incident response is preparation, which involves establishing policies, procedures, and resources to guide the organization's response to security incidents. CLI commands such as aws iam create-policy allow organizations to create IAM policies defining access controls and permissions for incident response teams, while aws ssm put-parameter enables the storage of critical incident response documentation, such as runbooks or contact lists, in AWS Systems Manager Parameter Store for easy access during emergencies. Additionally, organizations can use AWS CloudFormation with commands like aws cloudformation create-stack to automate the deployment of incident response infrastructure, including virtual private clouds (VPCs), security groups, and monitoring tools. Another crucial aspect of incident response is detection and analysis, where organizations leverage monitoring and logging solutions to identify suspicious activities and security breaches. CLI commands such as aws cloudtrail create-trail enable organizations to create CloudTrail trails to log API activity across their AWS accounts, while aws guardduty create-detector allows for the creation of GuardDuty detectors to continuously monitor for malicious behavior and unauthorized access.

Moreover, organizations can use AWS Lambda with commands like aws lambda create-function to deploy serverless functions for real-time analysis of log data and the generation of alerts based on predefined security rules. Additionally, organizations should prioritize containment and eradication to prevent further damage and restore affected systems to a secure state. CLI commands such as aws ec2 describe-instances enable incident response teams to gather information about compromised EC2 instances, while aws rds describe-db-instances provides details about compromised RDS database instances. Furthermore, organizations can use AWS Config with commands like aws config start-remediation-execution to automate the remediation of non-compliant resources and enforce security controls across their cloud environments. Additionally, organizations must conduct thorough forensic investigations to determine the root cause of security incidents and gather evidence for potential legal proceedings. CLI commands such as aws cloudwatchlogs create-log-group enable organizations to create log groups in CloudWatch Logs to store application and system logs for analysis, while aws s3api get-object allows for the retrieval of forensic artifacts stored in Amazon S3 buckets. Moreover, organizations can use AWS Security Hub with commands like aws securityhub enable-security-hub to aggregate and analyze security findings from multiple AWS services, providing a centralized view of security posture and enabling proactive threat detection and response. Furthermore, organizations should prioritize communication and collaboration among incident response teams, stakeholders, and external partners to ensure a coordinated and effective response to security incidents. CLI commands such as aws organizations invite-account-to-organization enable organizations to invite external parties to collaborate within an AWS Organization, while aws ssm send-command allows for the execution of commands on remote instances using AWS Systems Manager Run Command. Additionally, organizations can use AWS Chatbot with commands like aws chatbot create-connection to integrate AWS services with messaging platforms such as Slack or Microsoft Teams, enabling real-time communication and collaboration during incident response efforts. In conclusion, incident response and forensic investigation best practices are essential for organizations to effectively detect, contain, and mitigate security incidents in cloud environments. CLI commands provide incident response teams with the tools needed to automate response processes, gather evidence, and collaborate with stakeholders, enabling organizations to minimize the impact of security breaches and protect their assets and data.

Chapter 10: Exploring Future Trends and Innovations in Cloud Security

Quantum computing represents a paradigm shift in computing power, promising exponential increases in processing speed and capabilities compared to classical computers. CLI commands are not directly applicable to quantum computing but understanding its implications for cloud security is essential for organizations operating in the digital age. One significant implication of quantum computing for cloud security is its potential to break widely used encryption algorithms, such as RSA and ECC, which rely on the difficulty of factoring large numbers or solving discrete logarithm problems. While traditional encryption algorithms are secure against classical computers, quantum computers could theoretically solve these mathematical problems much faster using algorithms like Shor's algorithm. As a result, sensitive data encrypted using these algorithms could become vulnerable to decryption by quantum adversaries, posing a significant risk to data confidentiality. To address this risk, organizations must prepare for the advent of quantum computing by transitioning to quantum-resistant encryption algorithms that are immune to attacks from quantum computers. CLI commands are not directly applicable in this context, but organizations can deploy quantum-resistant encryption algorithms such as lattice-based cryptography, hash-based cryptography, or code-based cryptography through software updates or cryptographic libraries. Another implication of quantum computing for cloud security is its potential to undermine the integrity of digital signatures, which are used to verify the authenticity and integrity of digital documents and communications. Digital signatures rely on the difficulty of solving certain mathematical problems, such as the discrete logarithm problem or the factorization of large numbers, which could be efficiently solved by quantum computers using algorithms like Grover's algorithm. As a result, digital signatures generated using traditional algorithms could be forged or tampered with by quantum adversaries, compromising the integrity and authenticity of digital transactions. To mitigate this risk, organizations must transition to quantum-resistant digital signature algorithms, such as hash-based signatures or multivariate polynomial signatures, which are not vulnerable to quantum attacks. CLI commands are not directly applicable in this context, but organizations can deploy quantum-resistant digital signature algorithms through software updates or cryptographic libraries. Additionally, quantum computing has the potential to enhance certain aspects of cloud security, such as cryptography and random number generation. Quantum key distribution (QKD) protocols leverage the principles of quantum mechanics to secure communication channels by detecting any attempt to eavesdrop on transmitted quantum information. CLI commands are not directly applicable in this context, but organizations can deploy QKD protocols using specialized hardware devices or quantum communication platforms to establish secure communication channels between cloud services and users. Furthermore, quantum random number generators (QRNGs) can generate truly random numbers based on the unpredictable outcomes of quantum measurements, which are essential for cryptographic operations and security-sensitive applications. CLI commands are not directly applicable in this context, but organizations can deploy QRNGs using quantum hardware devices or integrate QRNG services provided by cloud service providers into their applications and systems. Moreover, quantum computing could enable more robust and efficient security solutions for cloud environments through techniques such as quantum machine learning and quantum-resistant cryptography. Quantum machine learning algorithms leverage the computational power of quantum computers to analyze large datasets and identify patterns or anomalies that may indicate security threats or vulnerabilities. CLI commands are not directly applicable in this context, but organizations can deploy quantum machine learning algorithms using quantum computing platforms or cloud-based quantum simulators to enhance threat detection and response capabilities. Additionally, quantum-resistant cryptography aims to develop cryptographic algorithms that remain secure against attacks from both classical and quantum computers, ensuring long-term protection for sensitive data and communications in cloud environments. CLI commands are not directly applicable in this context, but organizations can deploy quantum-resistant cryptography through software updates or cryptographic libraries to safeguard their cloud infrastructure and assets. In conclusion, quantum computing presents both challenges and opportunities for cloud security, requiring organizations to adapt their security strategies and technologies to mitigate emerging risks and capitalize on new capabilities.CLI commands are not directly applicable to quantum computing deployment, but understanding its implications for cloud security is crucial for organizations to stay ahead of evolving threats and maintain the confidentiality, integrity, and availability of their data and systems in the quantum era.

Emerging technologies are continually reshaping the landscape of cloud security, introducing both new opportunities and challenges for organizations navigating the digital landscape. CLI commands can play a vital role in deploying and managing these technologies within cloud environments, ensuring robust security postures and effective risk management strategies. One such emerging technology is artificial intelligence (AI), which is revolutionizing the way organizations detect, prevent, and respond to security threats in the cloud. CLI commands such as aws sagemaker create-endpoint enable organizations to deploy AI-powered threat detection models, leveraging machine learning algorithms to analyze vast amounts of data and identify anomalous behavior indicative of potential security breaches. Additionally, AI-driven security orchestration and automation platforms can streamline incident response workflows, allowing organizations to mitigate threats quickly and efficiently. Another emerging technology with a significant impact on cloud security is blockchain, which offers decentralized and tamper-resistant data storage and transaction capabilities. CLI commands such as ethereum-cli enable organizations to deploy blockchain-based smart contracts and decentralized applications (DApps) on cloud platforms, ensuring data integrity and immutability through cryptographic hashing and consensus mechanisms. By leveraging blockchain technology, organizations can enhance data privacy and transparency while reducing the risk of data tampering and unauthorized access. Moreover, edge computing is emerging as a critical technology for improving the performance and scalability of cloud-based applications and services. CLI commands such as aws iot create-device enable organizations to deploy edge computing devices and sensors, distributing computational workloads closer to the point of data generation and reducing latency for real-time applications. However, the proliferation of edge devices also introduces new security challenges, such as increased attack surface and limited security capabilities at the edge. To address these challenges, organizations must implement robust security measures, such as network segmentation, encryption, and device authentication, to protect edge computing infrastructure and data. Additionally, quantum computing is poised to revolutionize cryptographic algorithms and protocols, posing both opportunities and challenges for cloud security. CLI commands such as aws braket create-quantum-task enable organizations to access quantum computing resources through cloud services, allowing them to explore quantum-resistant encryption algorithms and develop strategies to mitigate the potential impact of quantum attacks on traditional cryptographic systems. By staying abreast of emerging technologies and their implications for cloud security, organizations can proactively adapt their security strategies and technologies to mitigate emerging risks and capitalize on new opportunities. Moreover, the Internet of Things (IoT) is transforming the way organizations collect, process, and analyze data in the cloud, enabling new applications and services across various industries. CLI commands such as aws iot create-topic-rule enable organizations to configure IoT devices and define rules for processing and routing data to cloud services, facilitating real-time monitoring and analysis of IoT data streams. However, the rapid proliferation of IoT devices also introduces new security challenges, such as device vulnerabilities, data privacy concerns, and network congestion. To address these challenges, organizations must implement robust IoT security measures, such as device authentication, encryption, and intrusion detection, to protect against cyber threats and ensure the integrity and confidentiality of IoT data. Additionally, serverless computing is gaining traction as a cost-effective and scalable alternative to traditional cloud infrastructure, enabling organizations to deploy and run applications without managing servers or infrastructure. CLI commands such as aws lambda create-function enable organizations to deploy serverless functions on cloud platforms, automating tasks and workflows while reducing operational overhead. However, serverless computing also introduces new security considerations, such as function-level permissions, resource isolation, and event-driven architecture. To address these considerations, organizations must implement security best practices for serverless environments, such as least privilege access, function monitoring, and secure coding practices, to mitigate the risk of security vulnerabilities and breaches. In conclusion, emerging technologies are reshaping the cloud security landscape, offering new opportunities for innovation and efficiency while presenting new challenges for risk management and data protection. By leveraging CLI commands and implementing robust security measures, organizations can navigate the evolving threat landscape and safeguard their cloud infrastructure and data against emerging cyber threats and vulnerabilities.

BOOK 4

MASTERING NIST CLOUD SECURITY
CUTTING-EDGE TECHNIQUES AND CASE STUDIES FOR SECURITY PROFESSIONALS

ROB BOTWRIGHT

Chapter 1: Advanced NIST Framework Integration Strategies

Assessing organizational readiness for NIST integration is a crucial step in ensuring successful adoption and implementation of the NIST framework within an organization. CLI commands such as nmap or openvas can be used to conduct vulnerability assessments across the organization's network infrastructure, identifying potential security gaps and vulnerabilities that may need to be addressed before integrating the NIST framework. Additionally, organizations can leverage security assessment frameworks such as the Cybersecurity Maturity Model Certification (CMMC) or the Center for Internet Security (CIS) Controls to evaluate their current security posture and identify areas for improvement. Conducting a comprehensive risk assessment is another essential component of assessing organizational readiness for NIST integration. This involves identifying and prioritizing potential risks and threats to the organization's information assets, including data breaches, cyber attacks, and regulatory compliance violations. CLI commands such as nmap or nessus can be used to scan the organization's network and systems for vulnerabilities, while tools like OWASP ZAP can be used to assess web application security. Additionally, organizations can conduct penetration testing exercises to simulate real-world cyber attacks and identify weaknesses in their security defenses. In addition to technical assessments, organizations should also evaluate their policies, procedures, and governance structures to ensure alignment with NIST guidelines and best practices. This includes reviewing security policies, incident response plans, and employee training programs to ensure they adequately address the requirements outlined in the NIST framework. CLI commands such as grep or awk can be used to analyze log files and audit trails to identify areas of non-compliance or security incidents that may require further investigation. Furthermore, organizations should assess their internal capabilities and resources to determine if they have the necessary expertise and personnel to effectively implement the NIST framework. This may involve conducting skills assessments, training programs, or hiring external consultants with expertise in cybersecurity and compliance. Additionally, organizations should consider their budgetary constraints and resource availability when assessing their readiness for NIST integration. This includes evaluating the costs associated with implementing the necessary security controls, training programs, and ongoing maintenance and monitoring activities. CLI commands such as ansible or terraform can be used to automate the deployment and management of security controls and infrastructure, helping organizations streamline the implementation process and reduce operational overhead. Lastly, organizations should engage key stakeholders and decision-makers throughout the assessment process to ensure buy-in and support for NIST integration initiatives. This may involve conducting workshops, meetings, or presentations to educate stakeholders about the benefits of adopting the NIST framework and address any concerns or objections they may have. By taking a comprehensive and systematic approach to assessing organizational readiness for NIST integration, organizations can identify potential barriers and challenges early on and develop a roadmap for successful implementation and compliance.

Developing customized NIST implementation roadmaps is a critical endeavor for organizations seeking to align their cybersecurity practices with the NIST framework's guidelines and recommendations. CLI commands such as git can be used to create a repository for storing and versioning the roadmap documents, allowing for collaborative development and easy access by stakeholders. The first step in developing a customized NIST implementation roadmap is to conduct a comprehensive assessment of the organization's current cybersecurity posture and capabilities. This assessment should encompass a thorough review of existing policies, procedures, controls, and technologies to identify areas of strength and weakness. CLI commands such as nmap or openvas can be employed to conduct vulnerability scans and identify potential security gaps that need to be addressed. Additionally, organizations should consider their specific industry, regulatory requirements, and risk profile when developing their NIST implementation roadmap. This may involve conducting interviews or workshops with key stakeholders to gather input and insights into the organization's unique cybersecurity challenges and objectives. Once the assessment phase is complete, organizations can begin to define their strategic goals and objectives for NIST implementation. CLI commands such as ansible or terraform can be utilized to automate the deployment and configuration of security controls and infrastructure, helping organizations streamline the implementation process and reduce manual effort. Organizations should prioritize their goals based on risk severity, regulatory requirements, and business priorities, ensuring that resources are allocated effectively and efficiently. Furthermore, organizations should develop a detailed action plan for achieving each strategic goal, including specific tasks, timelines, responsibilities, and success criteria. CLI commands such as cron or task scheduler can be employed to schedule regular security assessments and audits, ensuring ongoing compliance with NIST guidelines and standards. Additionally, organizations should establish key performance indicators (KPIs) and metrics to measure progress and track the effectiveness of their NIST implementation efforts. This may include metrics such as vulnerability remediation rates, incident response times, and compliance audit results. By regularly monitoring and evaluating these metrics, organizations can identify areas for improvement and make necessary adjustments to their implementation roadmap. Collaboration and communication are essential throughout the development and execution of the NIST implementation roadmap. CLI commands such as git or svn can be used to facilitate collaboration among team members, allowing for the sharing of documents, code, and other resources. Additionally, organizations should establish regular checkpoints and review meetings to assess progress, address challenges, and make course corrections as needed. Furthermore, organizations should communicate regularly with key stakeholders and decision-makers to ensure alignment with business objectives and priorities. This may involve providing regular updates, reports, and presentations on the status of NIST implementation efforts and the impact on overall cybersecurity posture. Finally, organizations should continuously monitor and evaluate the effectiveness of their NIST implementation roadmap and make adjustments as needed to address emerging threats, regulatory changes, and evolving business needs. By taking a proactive and iterative approach to NIST implementation, organizations can strengthen their cybersecurity defenses and reduce the risk of data breaches and cyber attacks.

Chapter 2: Cloud Security Architecture Design Patterns

Implementing microservices-based architectures for cloud security is becoming increasingly popular among organizations seeking more flexible, scalable, and resilient solutions. CLI commands such as docker-compose can be used to define and deploy microservices-based applications, allowing for easier management and orchestration of containerized services. Microservices architecture breaks down monolithic applications into smaller, independent services, each responsible for specific functions or features. By containerizing these services using tools like Docker or Kubernetes, organizations can achieve greater agility and scalability in their cloud environments. This approach also enables more efficient resource utilization, as services can be scaled independently based on demand. Furthermore, microservices architecture promotes modularity and reusability, making it easier to update and maintain individual components without impacting the entire system. Deploying microservices-based architectures for cloud security requires careful planning and consideration of various factors, including security, performance, and reliability. Organizations should conduct a thorough risk assessment to identify potential security vulnerabilities and threats associated with microservices deployment. CLI commands such as nmap or nessus can be used to scan for vulnerabilities in containerized environments and identify areas for improvement. Additionally, organizations should implement robust security controls and best practices to protect their microservices from unauthorized access, data breaches, and other cyber threats. This may include network segmentation, encryption, access controls, and regular security audits. Moreover, organizations should prioritize the use of secure coding practices and vulnerability management techniques to ensure that microservices are developed and maintained with security in mind. This includes conducting code reviews, implementing secure coding guidelines, and using automated testing tools to identify and remediate security issues early in the development lifecycle.

In addition to security considerations, organizations must also address performance and reliability concerns when implementing microservices-based architectures for cloud security. CLI commands such as curl or ab can be used to test the performance of microservices and identify potential bottlenecks or performance issues. Organizations should also implement monitoring and logging mechanisms to track the health and performance of their microservices in real-time. This includes collecting and analyzing metrics such as response times, error rates, and resource utilization to identify performance bottlenecks and optimize system performance. Furthermore, organizations should design their microservices architectures with fault tolerance and resiliency in mind, ensuring that individual services can fail gracefully without impacting the overall system. This may involve implementing redundancy, failover mechanisms, and automated recovery processes to minimize downtime and maintain service availability. When deploying microservices-based architectures for cloud security, organizations should also consider the impact on their existing infrastructure and workflows. CLI commands such as terraform or ansible can be used to automate the deployment and configuration of microservices infrastructure, making it easier to manage and scale cloud-based security solutions. Additionally, organizations should provide training and support for their IT teams to ensure they have the necessary skills and knowledge to manage and maintain microservices-based architectures effectively. This may include providing training on containerization technologies, orchestration tools, and cloud security best practices. Lastly, organizations should regularly evaluate and update their microservices architectures to address evolving security threats, technology advancements, and business requirements. By taking a proactive and iterative approach to microservices implementation, organizations can build more secure, scalable, and resilient cloud security solutions that meet the needs of their business and customers.

Leveraging Infrastructure as Code (IaC) for security architecture deployment offers numerous benefits in modern cloud environments. CLI commands such as Terraform or CloudFormation enable organizations to define and provision infrastructure using code, automating the deployment process and ensuring consistency across environments. By treating infrastructure as code, organizations can easily manage and version control their security configurations, reducing the risk of misconfigurations and human errors. With IaC, security configurations can be defined using declarative code, allowing organizations to specify the desired state of their infrastructure and automatically enforce security best practices. This approach facilitates compliance with security standards and regulations, as security policies can be codified and audited alongside other infrastructure components. Additionally, IaC enables organizations to implement security controls at scale, automatically provisioning and configuring resources according to predefined security templates and blueprints. This not only saves time and effort but also improves security posture by ensuring consistent enforcement of security policies across the entire infrastructure. Furthermore, IaC promotes collaboration and knowledge sharing among security and development teams, as code-based infrastructure configurations can be easily shared, reviewed, and modified using version control systems such as Git. This fosters a culture of DevSecOps, where security is integrated into the development and deployment process from the outset. When deploying security architecture using IaC, organizations should follow best practices to ensure the effectiveness and reliability of their implementations. This includes modularizing infrastructure code into reusable components, enabling organizations to standardize and streamline their security configurations across multiple environments. Moreover, organizations should leverage parameterization and variable management features in IaC tools to dynamically customize security configurations based on specific requirements and environments. Additionally, organizations should implement automated testing and validation processes to ensure the correctness and integrity of their infrastructure code, including security-related configurations. CLI commands such as Packer or Ansible can be used to automate the creation and provisioning of golden images and security-hardened configurations, reducing the attack surface and minimizing vulnerabilities in cloud environments. Organizations should also implement continuous integration and continuous deployment (CI/CD) pipelines for their infrastructure code, enabling them to automatically build, test, and deploy changes to their security configurations in a controlled and repeatable manner. This ensures that security updates and patches are applied promptly and consistently, reducing the risk of security breaches and data exposures. Furthermore, organizations should monitor and audit their infrastructure code and security configurations regularly to identify and remediate any misconfigurations or security vulnerabilities. CLI commands such as AWS Config or Terraform Cloud can be used to track changes to infrastructure configurations and detect drift from desired state, enabling organizations to enforce security policies and maintain compliance over time. In summary, leveraging Infrastructure as Code for security architecture deployment offers organizations a powerful and scalable approach to managing and enforcing security policies in cloud environments. By treating security configurations as code, organizations can automate the deployment process, ensure consistency across environments, and improve collaboration between security and development teams. However, organizations must follow best practices and implement robust testing and validation processes to ensure the reliability and effectiveness of their IaC-based security implementations. With careful planning and execution, IaC can help organizations achieve a higher level of security and compliance in their cloud deployments.

Chapter 3: Advanced Cloud Risk Assessment and Management

Conducting comprehensive threat modeling exercises is crucial for identifying and mitigating potential security risks in software systems. These exercises involve systematically analyzing the system architecture, identifying potential threats, and evaluating the effectiveness of existing security controls. Using CLI commands like Microsoft Threat Modeling Tool or OWASP Threat Dragon, security teams can facilitate these exercises by creating visual representations of the system architecture and mapping out potential threats. The first step in conducting a threat modeling exercise is to define the scope and objectives of the analysis. This involves identifying the assets, processes, and data flows within the system that need to be protected. Security teams can use CLI commands like nmap or dig to gather information about the system architecture and identify potential entry points for attackers. Once the scope is defined, the next step is to create a threat model that represents the system architecture and its components. This can be done using graphical tools or text-based diagrams, depending on the complexity of the system. Security teams should consider all possible attack vectors, including external threats such as hackers and malware, as well as insider threats and system vulnerabilities. CLI commands like nmap or Burp Suite can be used to conduct network scans and identify potential vulnerabilities in the system. After creating the threat model, the next step is to identify and prioritize potential threats. This involves brainstorming potential attack scenarios and assessing the likelihood and impact of each threat. Security teams can use techniques like threat trees or attack trees to systematically analyze each threat and its potential consequences. CLI commands like Metasploit or Nessus can be used to simulate attacks and assess the effectiveness of existing security controls. Once the threats are identified and prioritized, the next step is to develop mitigation strategies to address them. This may involve implementing additional security controls, updating software patches, or redesigning system architecture to minimize exposure to potential threats. CLI commands like iptables or firewalld can be used to configure network-level security controls and restrict access to vulnerable services. It's essential to involve stakeholders from across the organization in the threat modeling process to ensure that all relevant perspectives are considered. This may include representatives from IT, development, operations, and business units. By collaborating with stakeholders, security teams can gain valuable insights into potential threats and develop more effective mitigation strategies. Throughout the threat modeling process, it's essential to document findings and decisions to ensure that the results are effectively communicated and actionable. This may involve creating formal threat modeling reports or documentation that outlines the identified threats, mitigation strategies, and recommendations for improvement. CLI commands like Markdown or AsciiDoc can be used to create documentation in a structured and easily shareable format. After completing the threat modeling exercise, it's essential to review and update the threat model regularly to account for changes in the system architecture or the threat landscape. Threat modeling is an ongoing process that requires continuous vigilance and adaptation to remain effective. By regularly reviewing and updating the threat model, organizations can ensure that their security controls remain robust and resilient in the face of evolving threats. In conclusion, conducting comprehensive threat modeling exercises is a critical aspect of modern cybersecurity practices. By systematically analyzing system architecture, identifying potential threats, and developing mitigation strategies, organizations can proactively defend against security breaches and protect their valuable assets. CLI commands and tools play a crucial role in facilitating these exercises, enabling security teams to visualize system architecture, assess potential threats, and test the effectiveness of security controls. Through collaboration and ongoing vigilance, organizations can strengthen their security posture and mitigate the risks posed by ever-evolving cyber threats.

Integrating risk management into agile cloud environments is essential for organizations seeking to maintain robust security posture while embracing the flexibility and scalability of cloud technologies. In agile development methodologies, software development occurs in iterative cycles, with frequent updates and releases. CLI commands like Jira or Trello can be used to manage agile development processes and track the progress of development tasks. However, the rapid pace of development in agile environments can pose challenges for traditional risk management practices, which often rely on a more linear and structured approach. One approach to integrating risk management into agile environments is to incorporate risk assessment activities into each iteration of the development cycle. This involves identifying potential risks and vulnerabilities early in the development process and addressing them incrementally as part of ongoing development activities. CLI commands like OWASP ZAP or Nmap can be used to conduct automated security scans and identify potential vulnerabilities in the codebase. Another important aspect of integrating risk management into agile environments is fostering collaboration and communication between development, operations, and security teams. By involving all relevant stakeholders in the risk management process, organizations can ensure that security considerations are integrated into all stages of the development lifecycle. CLI commands like Slack or Microsoft Teams can be used to facilitate communication and collaboration between teams, allowing them to share information and coordinate efforts effectively. Additionally, organizations can leverage tools and technologies that support automated risk assessment and mitigation processes. CLI commands like Ansible or Terraform can be used to automate security configuration and deployment tasks, ensuring that security controls are consistently applied across the entire infrastructure. By automating routine security tasks, organizations can free up time and resources to focus on more strategic risk management activities. Another approach to integrating risk management into agile environments is to adopt a risk-based approach to prioritizing development tasks. This involves identifying the most critical risks and vulnerabilities and prioritizing development efforts to address them first. CLI commands like Git or GitHub can be used to manage code repositories and track changes to the codebase, allowing organizations to prioritize development tasks based on their impact on overall risk posture. Additionally, organizations can leverage threat modeling techniques to systematically identify and prioritize potential risks and vulnerabilities in the software architecture. CLI commands like OWASP Threat Dragon or Microsoft Threat Modeling Tool can be used to create visual representations of the system architecture and map out potential threats and attack vectors. By incorporating threat modeling into the development process, organizations can proactively identify and address security risks before they manifest in production environments.

Another important aspect of integrating risk management into agile environments is fostering a culture of security awareness and accountability within the organization. This involves providing ongoing training and education to development teams on security best practices and promoting a shared responsibility for security throughout the organization. CLI commands like OWASP Juice Shop or Damn Vulnerable Web Application (DVWA) can be used to provide hands-on training and practice opportunities for developers to learn about common security vulnerabilities and how to mitigate them. Additionally, organizations can implement security champions programs, where designated individuals within each development team take on additional responsibilities for promoting security awareness and best practices. By empowering developers to take ownership of security within their teams, organizations can foster a culture of security that extends beyond the confines of traditional security roles. In conclusion, integrating risk management into agile cloud environments is essential for organizations seeking to balance the need for speed and agility with the imperative of maintaining robust security posture. By incorporating risk assessment activities into each iteration of the development cycle, fostering collaboration and communication between development, operations, and security teams, adopting automated risk assessment and mitigation processes, prioritizing development tasks based on risk, leveraging threat modeling techniques, and promoting a culture of security awareness and accountability, organizations can effectively manage security risks in agile cloud environments.CLI commands can play a crucial role in facilitating these efforts by providing tools and technologies that support agile development practices and enable organizations to automate routine security tasks, identify and prioritize development tasks, and foster collaboration and communication between teams. Through a combination of people, processes, and technology, organizations can achieve the dual objectives of rapid innovation and strong security in agile cloud environments.

Chapter 4: Implementing Continuous Compliance Monitoring

Automating compliance checks with DevOps pipelines is a critical aspect of modern software development practices, allowing organizations to ensure that their applications adhere to regulatory requirements and internal policies throughout the development lifecycle. CLI commands like Jenkins or GitLab CI/CD play a pivotal role in setting up and managing DevOps pipelines, enabling organizations to automate various stages of the software delivery process, including compliance checks. One key benefit of automating compliance checks with DevOps pipelines is the ability to integrate security and compliance into the development process from the outset, rather than treating them as separate and distinct activities. This shift-left approach enables organizations to identify and address compliance issues early in the development lifecycle, reducing the risk of costly rework and delays later on. By automating compliance checks as part of the CI/CD pipeline, organizations can ensure that every code change undergoes rigorous scrutiny for compliance with regulatory requirements, security standards, and internal policies before being deployed to production. CLI commands like SonarQube or Checkmarx can be integrated into DevOps pipelines to perform static code analysis and identify potential compliance issues, such as insecure coding practices or violations of coding standards. Additionally, organizations can leverage infrastructure as code (IaC) tools like Terraform or AWS CloudFormation to automate the provisioning and configuration of cloud resources in a compliant manner. By codifying infrastructure configurations, organizations can ensure that their cloud environments adhere to predefined security and compliance policies, reducing the risk of misconfigurations and vulnerabilities. Another benefit of automating compliance checks with DevOps pipelines is the ability to enforce consistency and standardization across development teams and projects. By defining compliance rules and policies as code, organizations can ensure that all applications adhere to the same set of standards and best practices, regardless of the development team or project involved. CLI commands like Ansible or Chef can be used to automate the enforcement of compliance policies across infrastructure and application configurations, ensuring that deviations from established standards are quickly identified and remediated. Furthermore, automating compliance checks with DevOps pipelines enables organizations to achieve greater visibility and traceability into the compliance status of their applications and environments. By integrating compliance checks into the CI/CD pipeline, organizations can generate automated reports and audit trails that provide real-time insights into the compliance posture of their software projects. CLI commands like Splunk or ELK Stack can be used to aggregate and analyze compliance data from various sources, providing stakeholders with actionable insights into areas of non-compliance and opportunities for improvement. Additionally, organizations can implement automated notification mechanisms to alert relevant stakeholders to compliance violations or security incidents as they occur, enabling timely remediation actions to be taken. One common challenge organizations face when automating compliance checks with DevOps pipelines is ensuring that the compliance rules and policies codified in the pipeline accurately reflect regulatory requirements and industry standards. To address this challenge, organizations should regularly review and update their compliance rules and policies to ensure they remain current and relevant in the face of evolving regulatory landscapes and emerging security threats. CLI commands like GitHub Actions or Bitbucket Pipelines provide mechanisms for versioning and managing pipeline configurations, enabling organizations to track changes to compliance rules and policies over time and maintain an audit trail of compliance-related activities. Additionally, organizations can leverage automated testing frameworks like Gherkin or Selenium to validate compliance rules and policies as part of the CI/CD pipeline, ensuring that changes to pipeline configurations do not inadvertently introduce compliance issues. Another challenge organizations may encounter when automating compliance checks with DevOps pipelines is the need to balance speed and agility with security and compliance requirements. While automation can streamline the compliance process and accelerate software delivery, organizations must ensure that automated checks are thorough and comprehensive to effectively mitigate compliance risks. CLI commands like CircleCI or Travis CI offer features for parallelizing and distributing compliance checks across multiple environments, allowing organizations to achieve faster feedback loops without sacrificing the quality or integrity of compliance checks.

Additionally, organizations can implement automated gating mechanisms in their DevOps pipelines to prevent non-compliant code changes from progressing to subsequent stages of the pipeline until remediation actions have been taken. By integrating compliance checks into the CI/CD pipeline and leveraging automation tools and techniques, organizations can achieve greater efficiency, consistency, and reliability in their compliance efforts while supporting the rapid delivery of secure and compliant software solutions.

Leveraging machine learning for dynamic compliance monitoring represents a cutting-edge approach to ensuring adherence to regulatory requirements and security standards in dynamic and rapidly evolving environments. CLI commands such as TensorFlow or Scikit-learn can be instrumental in implementing machine learning algorithms for compliance monitoring, enabling organizations to analyze vast amounts of data and detect compliance violations in real-time. One of the key advantages of using machine learning for dynamic compliance monitoring is its ability to adapt and evolve alongside changing regulatory landscapes and organizational requirements. By training machine learning models on historical compliance data and continuously updating them with new information, organizations can develop predictive capabilities for identifying potential compliance issues before they occur. Moreover, machine learning algorithms can analyze complex patterns and relationships within compliance data, enabling organizations to uncover insights and trends that may not be apparent through traditional methods. This allows organizations to proactively address compliance risks and strengthen their overall security posture. Deploying machine learning for dynamic compliance monitoring begins with the collection and preprocessing of relevant data sources, including audit logs, access records, and configuration files, among others. CLI commands like grep, awk, or sed can be used to extract and transform raw data into a format suitable for analysis by machine learning algorithms. Once the data has been prepared, organizations can use machine learning frameworks such as TensorFlow or PyTorch to train predictive models on historical compliance data. During the training process, organizations must ensure that the machine learning models are provided with labeled data indicating instances of compliance and non-compliance, allowing them to learn to distinguish between the two. Once the machine learning models have been trained, they can be deployed to monitor ongoing compliance in real-time. This involves feeding new data streams into the models and using their predictions to identify potential compliance violations as they occur. CLI commands such as cron or systemd can be used to schedule regular executions of the machine learning models, ensuring that compliance monitoring remains continuous and uninterrupted. Additionally, organizations can integrate machine learning models into existing monitoring and alerting systems to automatically notify relevant stakeholders of compliance issues detected by the models. This allows organizations to respond quickly to compliance violations and take appropriate remediation actions to address them. One of the key challenges organizations may face when leveraging machine learning for dynamic compliance monitoring is the need for high-quality, labeled training data. Without sufficient and accurate training data, machine learning models may struggle to generalize to new data and accurately predict compliance violations. To address this challenge, organizations should invest in data quality assurance processes and collaborate with subject matter experts to ensure that training data accurately reflects real-world compliance scenarios. Additionally, organizations can use techniques such as data augmentation and synthetic data generation to supplement their training datasets and improve the robustness of their machine learning models. Another challenge organizations may encounter is the interpretability and explainability of machine learning models used for compliance monitoring. Complex machine learning algorithms such as deep neural networks may produce opaque or inscrutable predictions, making it difficult for stakeholders to understand how decisions are being made. To address this challenge, organizations should prioritize the use of interpretable machine learning techniques such as decision trees or logistic regression, which produce transparent models that can be easily understood and interpreted by humans. Additionally, organizations can use techniques such as feature importance analysis or model explanation frameworks to gain insights into the factors driving model predictions and identify areas for improvement. Despite these challenges, the benefits of leveraging machine learning for dynamic compliance monitoring are significant. By automating compliance monitoring and detection processes, organizations can reduce the burden on human analysts and improve the scalability and efficiency of their compliance efforts. Moreover, machine learning algorithms can adapt and evolve over time, allowing organizations to stay ahead of emerging compliance risks and regulatory requirements. Ultimately, the integration of machine learning into compliance monitoring processes represents a powerful opportunity for organizations to enhance their security posture, mitigate compliance risks, and build trust with customers and stakeholders.

Chapter 5: Advanced Threat Detection and Response in Cloud Environments

Implementing behavior-based threat detection mechanisms is essential in modern cybersecurity practices to combat increasingly sophisticated cyber threats. CLI commands like tcpdump or Wireshark are indispensable for capturing network traffic, a fundamental step in behavior-based threat detection. Analyzing network traffic patterns can reveal abnormal behavior indicative of potential threats, such as unusual communication patterns or unauthorized access attempts. Behavioral analysis extends beyond network traffic to encompass user behavior, application behavior, and system behavior, providing a holistic view of potential threats. CLI commands such as ps or top are used to monitor processes and system activities, allowing security teams to detect anomalous behavior indicative of malicious activity. By continuously monitoring system logs and event data, organizations can identify deviations from normal behavior that may signal a security breach or intrusion. Deploying behavior-based threat detection mechanisms involves integrating various tools and technologies into the organization's existing security infrastructure. CLI commands such as grep or awk can be used to parse and analyze log files, extracting relevant information for behavioral analysis. Organizations must also leverage advanced analytics platforms and machine learning algorithms to process and analyze large volumes of data for suspicious patterns and anomalies. These platforms enable automated threat detection and response, augmenting the capabilities of security teams and reducing response times to security incidents. Machine learning algorithms can be trained on historical data to identify patterns of behavior associated with known threats, enabling organizations to proactively detect and mitigate emerging threats. Additionally, organizations can use anomaly detection techniques to identify deviations from expected behavior, flagging potential security risks for further investigation. Behavioral analysis can also be applied to user activity, helping organizations detect insider threats and unauthorized access attempts. By monitoring user behavior across multiple dimensions, including login activity, file access patterns, and application usage, organizations can identify suspicious behavior indicative of insider threats or compromised accounts. Behavioral analysis can also help organizations detect and respond to sophisticated cyber attacks, such as advanced persistent threats (APTs) and zero-day exploits. By analyzing the behavior of malware and other malicious code, security teams can identify and mitigate threats before they cause significant damage. Furthermore, behavior-based threat detection mechanisms enable organizations to adapt to evolving threats and attack techniques. CLI commands such as iptables or firewalld can be used to configure network security policies based on observed behavior, blocking or restricting access to suspicious IP addresses or malicious domains. Continuous monitoring and refinement of threat detection mechanisms are essential to ensure ongoing effectiveness in detecting and mitigating cybersecurity threats. By regularly updating threat models and refining detection algorithms, organizations can stay ahead of emerging threats and protect their critical assets from cyber attacks. Moreover, organizations must establish clear processes and protocols for responding to security incidents identified through behavior-based threat detection. CLI commands such as curl or wget can be used to retrieve threat intelligence feeds and update security controls in real-time, enhancing the organization's ability to detect and respond to emerging threats. Collaboration with industry peers and sharing of threat intelligence are also critical components of effective behavior-based threat detection. By participating in information sharing and analysis centers (ISACs) and threat intelligence sharing platforms, organizations can gain access to valuable insights and indicators of compromise (IOCs) to enhance their threat detection capabilities. In conclusion, implementing behavior-based threat detection mechanisms is essential for organizations to detect and mitigate cybersecurity threats effectively. By leveraging CLI commands, advanced analytics, and machine learning algorithms, organizations can analyze diverse data sources and identify suspicious behavior indicative of potential security breaches. Continuous monitoring, refinement, and collaboration are essential to ensure the ongoing effectiveness of behavior-based threat detection in the face of evolving cyber threats. Orchestrating incident response across cloud platforms is a critical aspect of modern cybersecurity practices, given the widespread adoption of cloud services by organizations. CLI commands like aws-cli or gcloud are essential for managing cloud resources and orchestrating incident response activities in multi-cloud environments. Incident response orchestration involves coordinating and automating the response efforts across different cloud platforms to effectively detect, contain, and mitigate security incidents. By integrating various security tools and technologies into a unified orchestration framework, organizations can streamline incident response workflows and improve their overall security posture. Centralized orchestration platforms such as Security Orchestration, Automation, and Response (SOAR) systems play a vital role in orchestrating incident response across cloud platforms. CLI commands such as curl or wget can be used to interact with APIs exposed by SOAR platforms, enabling automation and integration with cloud services. These platforms provide a centralized dashboard for security teams to manage and coordinate incident response activities across multiple cloud environments. Incident response orchestration begins with the detection of security incidents, which can be triggered by alerts generated from various security monitoring tools deployed in the cloud environment. CLI commands like grep or awk are commonly used to parse and analyze log files, extracting relevant information for incident detection. Security Information and Event Management (SIEM) platforms are often deployed to aggregate and correlate security events from different cloud platforms, providing a centralized view of potential security threats. Upon detection of a security incident, the orchestration platform initiates a predefined response workflow, which may include automated actions such as isolating affected resources, blocking malicious IP addresses, or triggering notifications to security personnel. CLI commands such as iptables or firewall-cmd can be used to implement network security controls, such as blocking traffic from suspicious IP addresses or restricting access to compromised resources. Incident response playbooks are predefined sets of actions and procedures that guide security teams through the response process for specific types of security incidents. CLI commands like ansible or terraform are commonly used to automate playbook execution, enabling rapid and consistent response to security incidents across cloud platforms. Playbooks may include steps such as gathering evidence, containing the incident, eradicating malware, and restoring affected systems to a known good state. Incident response teams must regularly review and update playbooks to ensure they remain effective against evolving threats and attack techniques. Communication and collaboration are essential during incident response orchestration, especially in multi-cloud environments where multiple teams may be involved in the response effort. CLI commands such as ssh or scp can be used to securely communicate and share information between different teams and cloud platforms. Incident response platforms often include built-in collaboration features, such as chat rooms and incident timelines, to facilitate communication and coordination among team members. Timely and accurate communication is critical for ensuring that all stakeholders are informed about the incident's status and progress towards resolution. Post-incident analysis and lessons learned are essential for improving incident response processes and mitigating future security incidents. CLI commands such as grep or awk can be used to search and analyze historical data for insights into the incident's root cause and impact. Incident response teams should conduct thorough post-mortem reviews to identify gaps in their response procedures and opportunities for improvement. This may include updating playbooks, enhancing detection capabilities, or implementing additional security controls to prevent similar incidents from occurring in the future. Continuous monitoring and refinement of incident response processes are essential for maintaining an effective security posture in multi-cloud environments. CLI commands such as cron or systemctl can be used to schedule regular security audits and reviews, ensuring that incident response procedures remain up-to-date and aligned with the organization's security objectives. By orchestrating incident response across cloud platforms, organizations can improve their ability to detect, contain, and mitigate security incidents, ultimately enhancing their overall resilience to cyber threats.

Chapter 6: Securing Multi-Cloud and Hybrid Environments

Implementing centralized identity and access management (IAM) across multiple cloud environments is crucial for ensuring secure and efficient access control to resources. CLI commands such as aws iam or gcloud iam are essential for managing IAM configurations in cloud platforms like AWS or Google Cloud. Centralized IAM allows organizations to manage user identities, roles, and permissions from a single location, providing a unified approach to access control. This helps to streamline administration, enforce consistent security policies, and reduce the risk of unauthorized access across cloud platforms. One of the key components of centralized IAM is the use of directory services such as Active Directory or LDAP for user authentication and authorization. CLI commands like ldapsearch or dsquery can be used to interact with LDAP directories and perform user management tasks. By integrating cloud platforms with existing directory services, organizations can leverage existing user identities and access controls, simplifying the management of access policies across clouds. Role-based access control (RBAC) is another fundamental aspect of centralized IAM, allowing organizations to assign permissions to users based on their roles and responsibilities. CLI commands such as aws iam create-role or gcloud iam roles create are used to define roles and attach permissions to them in cloud environments. By implementing RBAC, organizations can ensure that users have the appropriate level of access to resources based on their job functions, reducing the risk of unauthorized access and data breaches. Single sign-on (SSO) is a critical feature of centralized IAM that enables users to access multiple cloud applications and services using a single set of credentials. CLI commands such as saml2aws or gcloud auth login can be used to authenticate users and obtain temporary credentials for accessing cloud resources via SSO. By implementing SSO, organizations can improve user experience, enhance security, and simplify access management across cloud platforms. Multi-factor authentication (MFA) is another essential security control that adds an extra layer of protection to user accounts by requiring users to provide multiple forms of verification. CLI commands like aws iam enable-mfa-device or gcloud auth login --enable-device-verification are used to enable MFA for IAM users in cloud environments. By implementing MFA, organizations can reduce the risk of unauthorized access due to compromised credentials and strengthen overall security posture across clouds. Identity federation is a technique used to establish trust relationships between different identity providers, allowing users to access resources across multiple domains without the need for separate authentication. CLI commands such as aws sts assume-role-with-saml or gcloud iam identity create are used to obtain temporary credentials for accessing resources in federated environments. By implementing identity federation, organizations can extend centralized IAM policies and controls to external partners, suppliers, and customers, enabling secure collaboration across cloud boundaries. Automated provisioning and deprovisioning of user accounts is essential for maintaining security and compliance in dynamic cloud environments. CLI commands like aws iam create-user or gcloud iam service-accounts create are used to automate the creation of user accounts and assign them appropriate roles and permissions. By integrating IAM with identity lifecycle management systems, organizations can streamline user onboarding and offboarding processes, ensuring that access rights are granted and revoked in a timely manner. Auditing and monitoring are critical aspects of centralized IAM that help organizations track user activities, detect suspicious behavior, and enforce compliance with security policies. CLI commands such as aws cloudtrail start-logging or gcloud logging logs list are used to enable logging and monitoring in cloud environments. By analyzing audit logs and monitoring user activity, organizations can identify security incidents, investigate root causes, and take appropriate remedial actions to mitigate risks. Continuous compliance management is essential for ensuring that IAM configurations remain aligned with regulatory requirements and industry best practices. CLI commands like aws config start-configuration-recorder or gcloud asset list are used to assess IAM configurations against predefined compliance rules and standards. By automating compliance checks and remediation actions, organizations can maintain a strong security posture and reduce the risk of non-compliance-related fines and penalties. In summary, implementing centralized IAM across clouds is essential for ensuring secure and efficient access control to resources in modern cloud environments. By leveraging directory services, RBAC, SSO, MFA, identity federation, automated provisioning, auditing, monitoring, and compliance management, organizations can establish a robust IAM framework that enhances security, simplifies administration, and enables seamless collaboration across cloud platforms.

Implementing cross-cloud data encryption strategies is crucial for safeguarding sensitive information across multiple cloud environments. CLI commands such as aws kms create-key or gcloud kms keys create are used to create encryption keys in cloud key management services. These encryption keys serve as the foundation for securing data at rest and in transit across clouds. By encrypting data before it is stored in the cloud, organizations can prevent unauthorized access and data breaches, even if the underlying storage infrastructure is compromised. Additionally, encrypting data in transit ensures that information remains protected as it travels between cloud environments and end users. One approach to implementing cross-cloud data encryption is to use client-side encryption, where data is encrypted on the client device before being uploaded to the cloud. CLI commands like openssl enc or gpg --encrypt can be used to encrypt files locally before transferring them to cloud storage services. By encrypting data at the client side, organizations can maintain full control over the encryption process and ensure that data remains protected throughout its lifecycle in the cloud. Another approach to cross-cloud data encryption is to leverage cloud-native encryption capabilities provided by cloud service providers. CLI commands such as aws s3 cp --sse or gcloud storage cp -k are used to upload files to cloud storage services with server-side encryption enabled. With server-side encryption, data is encrypted by the cloud provider using encryption keys managed by the provider's key management service. This approach simplifies encryption management and ensures consistent security across different cloud platforms. Additionally, many cloud providers offer encryption options for their networking services, such as virtual private clouds (VPCs) and virtual networks, to encrypt data in transit between cloud resources. CLI commands like aws ec2 create-vpc or gcloud compute networks create can be used to create encrypted VPCs or networks in AWS or Google Cloud, respectively. By encrypting network traffic between cloud resources, organizations can prevent eavesdropping and man-in-the-middle attacks, further enhancing data security in multi-cloud environments. Implementing encryption key management is a critical aspect of cross-cloud data encryption, as it ensures that encryption keys are securely stored, managed, and rotated over time. CLI commands such as aws kms create-alias or gcloud kms keyrings create are used to create key aliases or keyrings in cloud key management services, respectively. By centralizing key management in a dedicated key management service, organizations can enforce consistent encryption policies and maintain visibility and control over encryption keys across multiple cloud platforms. Additionally, implementing key rotation and key versioning practices helps to mitigate the risk of key compromise and ensure that encryption keys remain secure over time. Another important consideration when implementing cross-cloud data encryption is compliance with regulatory requirements and industry standards. CLI commands such as aws configservice put-config-rule or gcloud resource-manager org-policies can be used to define and enforce encryption-related compliance rules in AWS Config or Google Cloud Organization Policies, respectively. By aligning encryption practices with regulatory requirements such as GDPR, HIPAA, or PCI DSS, organizations can demonstrate compliance and minimize the risk of regulatory penalties and fines. Monitoring and auditing are essential components of cross-cloud data encryption, as they help organizations detect and respond to security incidents in a timely manner. CLI commands like aws cloudtrail start-logging or gcloud logging logs list are used to enable logging and monitoring in cloud environments. By analyzing audit logs and monitoring encryption-related metrics, organizations can identify security threats, investigate security incidents, and take appropriate remedial actions to mitigate risks. Additionally, implementing automated alerts and notifications helps to ensure that security teams are promptly notified of any suspicious activities or unauthorized access attempts related to data encryption. In summary, implementing cross-cloud data encryption strategies is essential for protecting sensitive information in multi-cloud environments. By leveraging client-side encryption, cloud-native encryption capabilities, encrypted networking services, encryption key management practices, compliance enforcement mechanisms, and monitoring and auditing controls, organizations can establish a robust encryption framework that enhances data security, ensures regulatory compliance, and mitigates the risk of data breaches across cloud platforms.

Chapter 7: Advanced Cloud Security Automation Techniques

Implementing self-healing security mechanisms in cloud environments is crucial for proactively identifying and mitigating security threats. CLI commands such as aws configure or gcloud auth login are used to authenticate and configure access to cloud services. These mechanisms leverage automation and artificial intelligence to detect anomalies, respond to incidents, and remediate security vulnerabilities in real time. By continuously monitoring cloud infrastructure, applications, and data, organizations can detect deviations from normal behavior that may indicate security breaches or malicious activities. Using machine learning algorithms, anomaly detection systems analyze vast amounts of data to identify patterns and trends indicative of potential security threats. Once anomalies are detected, automated responses can be triggered to mitigate risks and prevent further exploitation. For example, if abnormal network traffic is detected, self-healing security mechanisms can automatically isolate affected systems or block malicious IP addresses to contain the threat.

Implementing self-healing security mechanisms requires integration with existing security controls and workflows. CLI commands such as aws lambda create-function or gcloud functions deploy are used to deploy serverless functions that automate security responses. These functions can be triggered by alerts from intrusion detection systems, security information and event management (SIEM) solutions, or cloud monitoring services. By orchestrating security responses through automation, organizations can reduce the time to detect and respond to security incidents, minimizing the impact on business operations. Self-healing security mechanisms can also include automated patching and vulnerability remediation processes. CLI commands like aws systems-manager create-patch-baseline or gcloud compute instances update are used to create patch baselines and apply updates to cloud instances. By regularly scanning cloud resources for known vulnerabilities and applying patches automatically, organizations can reduce the attack surface and protect against known exploits. Additionally, self-healing security mechanisms can leverage configuration management tools to enforce security policies and ensure compliance with industry standards and regulatory requirements. CLI commands such as aws configservice put-config-rule or gcloud resource-manager org-policies are used to define and enforce security configurations in cloud environments. These configurations can include requirements for encryption, access controls, network segmentation, and other security best practices. By automating the enforcement of security policies, organizations can maintain consistent security posture across their cloud infrastructure. Another aspect of self-healing security is the use of container orchestration platforms like Kubernetes to automatically detect and respond to security threats in containerized environments. CLI commands such as kubectl apply or gcloud container clusters create are used to deploy Kubernetes clusters and manage containerized workloads. Kubernetes provides built-in features for monitoring container health, scaling resources, and rolling out updates, which can be leveraged to implement self-healing security mechanisms. For example, Kubernetes can automatically restart containers that fail health checks or deploy additional replicas to handle increased traffic or workload demand. Implementing self-healing security mechanisms also requires robust incident response and recovery processes. CLI commands such as aws cloudformation create-stack or gcloud deployment-manager deployments create are used to deploy infrastructure as code templates that define cloud resources and configurations. By codifying infrastructure and automating deployment processes, organizations can quickly restore services in the event of security incidents or system failures. Additionally, organizations should regularly test their self-healing security mechanisms through simulated security incidents and tabletop exercises. CLI commands like aws inspector start-assessment-run or gcloud compute ssh can be used to initiate vulnerability assessments and penetration tests in cloud environments. By identifying weaknesses in security controls and incident response procedures, organizations can iteratively improve their self-healing capabilities and enhance overall security posture. In summary, implementing self-healing security mechanisms in cloud environments is essential for proactively detecting and responding to security threats. By leveraging automation, machine learning, configuration management, container orchestration, and incident response processes, organizations can enhance resilience, minimize risk, and maintain continuous protection against evolving cyber threats.

Leveraging artificial intelligence (AI) for predictive

security analytics in the cloud is becoming increasingly vital as organizations seek proactive approaches to cyber defense. AI algorithms can analyze vast amounts of data to detect patterns and anomalies indicative of potential security threats. CLI commands such as aws sagemaker create-endpoint or gcloud ai-platform models deploy are used to deploy machine learning models that power predictive security analytics. These models can ingest data from various sources, including logs, network traffic, and endpoint telemetry, to identify abnormal behavior and potential indicators of compromise. By continuously monitoring cloud environments, AI-driven predictive analytics can help organizations stay ahead of emerging threats and prevent security incidents before they occur. Machine learning algorithms can learn from historical data to predict future security events and prioritize mitigation efforts accordingly. For example, AI models can analyze past cyberattacks to identify common attack vectors and predict the likelihood of similar incidents occurring in the future. By proactively addressing known vulnerabilities and weaknesses in security controls, organizations can reduce the risk of successful cyberattacks. Implementing AI-driven predictive security analytics requires robust data collection and preprocessing pipelines. CLI commands such as aws glue create-job or gcloud dataflow jobs run are used to create data processing jobs that extract, transform, and load (ETL) data into the AI model. These pipelines must ingest data from diverse sources, normalize it into a consistent format, and remove any noise or irrelevant information that could skew the analysis. Once the data is preprocessed, it is fed into the AI model for training and inference. Training AI models for predictive security analytics requires labeled datasets that represent both normal and malicious behavior. CLI commands such as aws sagemaker create-training-job or gcloud ai-platform jobs submit training are used to train machine learning models on cloud-based infrastructure. During the training process, the AI model learns to distinguish between normal and anomalous patterns in the data and to make predictions based on learned patterns. Once the model is trained, it can be deployed into production to analyze real-time data streams and generate predictive insights. Deploying AI models for predictive security analytics involves configuring endpoints or APIs that expose the model's inference capabilities. CLI commands such as aws sagemaker create-endpoint or gcloud ai-platform models deploy are used to deploy the model to scalable and reliable infrastructure that can handle production workloads. Once deployed, the model can receive input data from cloud-based applications, services, and devices and generate predictions in real time. These predictions can be used to trigger automated responses, such as blocking suspicious network traffic or alerting security analysts to potential threats. Integrating AI-driven predictive security analytics into existing security operations requires close collaboration between data scientists, security analysts, and IT operations teams. CLI commands such as aws organizations create-account or gcloud organizations add-iam-policy-binding are used to manage access controls and permissions for accessing data and deploying AI models. Security teams must work together to define use cases, gather data, train models, and operationalize predictive analytics within the organization's security infrastructure. Additionally, organizations must ensure that AI models are continuously monitored and updated to adapt to evolving threats and changing environmental conditions. CLI commands such as aws sagemaker update-endpoint or gcloud ai-platform versions update are used to update deployed models with new training data or retrain them with updated algorithms. By continuously improving AI-driven predictive security analytics, organizations can enhance their ability to detect and respond to cyber threats effectively. In summary, leveraging AI for predictive security analytics in the cloud enables organizations to proactively identify and mitigate security risks before they escalate into full-blown incidents. By harnessing the power of machine learning algorithms and cloud-based infrastructure, organizations can stay one step ahead of cyber adversaries and protect their sensitive data and assets from harm.

Chapter 8: Case Studies in Cloud Security Success Stories

Implementing Zero Trust architecture successfully in a large enterprise requires a comprehensive understanding of the underlying principles and careful planning to ensure effective deployment. CLI commands such as kubectl apply -f or terraform apply are commonly used to deploy Zero Trust components in cloud-native environments. Zero Trust architecture is based on the principle of assuming that every entity, both internal and external to the network, is untrusted and should not be granted unrestricted access. This approach contrasts with traditional perimeter-based security models that rely on network boundaries for protection. By adopting a Zero Trust mindset, organizations can strengthen their security posture and mitigate the risk of unauthorized access and data breaches. The first step in implementing Zero Trust architecture is to define trust boundaries and identify the critical assets and resources that need protection. CLI commands such as nmap or traceroute can be used to map out network dependencies and identify potential security vulnerabilities. Once the trust boundaries are established, organizations can begin to implement access controls and segmentation policies to enforce the principle of least privilege. This involves restricting access to resources based on the principle of need-to-know and implementing strong authentication mechanisms to verify the identity of users and devices. CLI commands such as iptables or Azure Network Security Groups are used to configure firewall rules and network segmentation policies that limit lateral movement within the network. Implementing Zero Trust architecture also requires organizations to adopt a holistic approach to security that encompasses both network and application-layer controls. This includes implementing encryption protocols such as TLS/SSL to protect data in transit and deploying intrusion detection and prevention systems (IDPS) to detect and block malicious activity. CLI commands such as openssl or certbot can be used to generate and manage SSL/TLS certificates for securing communication between applications and services. Additionally, organizations should implement strong identity and access management (IAM) controls to ensure that only authorized users and devices can access sensitive resources. This involves implementing multi-factor authentication (MFA) and role-based access control (RBAC) policies to enforce granular access controls and minimize the risk of privilege escalation. CLI commands such as aws iam create-role or gcloud iam service-accounts create are used to create IAM roles and service accounts that enforce access controls based on user roles and permissions. In addition to network and application-layer controls, organizations should also focus on endpoint security to protect devices and endpoints from compromise. This involves implementing endpoint protection platforms (EPP) and endpoint detection and response (EDR) solutions to detect and mitigate threats at the device level. CLI commands such as Microsoft Defender ATP or CrowdStrike Falcon can be used to deploy and manage endpoint security solutions that provide real-time threat detection and response capabilities. As part of the Zero Trust architecture implementation process, organizations should also establish continuous monitoring and auditing capabilities to detect and respond to security incidents in real time. This involves implementing security information and event management (SIEM) systems and log management solutions to aggregate and analyze security logs and telemetry data from across the enterprise. CLI commands such as Splunk or Elasticsearch can be used to deploy SIEM solutions that provide centralized visibility into security events and anomalies. Additionally, organizations should conduct regular security assessments and penetration testing exercises to identify and remediate security vulnerabilities before they can be exploited by attackers. CLI commands such as Nessus or OpenVAS can be used to perform vulnerability scans and security assessments that identify weaknesses in the organization's security posture. By following these best practices and leveraging CLI commands where applicable, organizations can successfully implement Zero Trust architecture in a large enterprise and strengthen their security posture against evolving cyber threats. Achieving regulatory compliance in highly regulated industries with cloud solutions is a complex process that requires careful planning and execution. Compliance requirements vary depending on the industry and jurisdiction, with regulations such as HIPAA, GDPR, PCI DSS, and SOX governing data protection, privacy, and security standards. Organizations must ensure that their cloud solutions adhere to these regulations to avoid penalties and legal consequences. CLI commands such as aws configure or az login are often used to authenticate and access cloud services when deploying compliance measures. One of the first steps in achieving regulatory compliance is conducting a thorough assessment of the organization's current compliance posture and identifying gaps in existing policies and procedures. This involves reviewing regulatory requirements and conducting risk assessments to determine the level of compliance needed. CLI commands such as nmap or OpenVAS can be used to perform vulnerability scans and identify security weaknesses that may impact compliance. Once the current compliance posture is understood, organizations can begin to implement the necessary controls and measures to achieve compliance with relevant regulations. This may involve implementing encryption protocols such as TLS/SSL to protect sensitive data in transit and at rest. CLI commands such as openssl or certbot can be used to generate and manage SSL/TLS certificates for securing communication between applications and services. Additionally, organizations must implement access controls and authentication mechanisms to ensure that only authorized users have access to sensitive data and resources. CLI commands such as IAM policies or Active Directory group policies can be used to enforce role-based access control (RBAC) policies that restrict access based on user roles and permissions. Another important aspect of achieving regulatory compliance is ensuring that data is stored and processed in accordance with regulatory requirements. This may involve implementing data classification policies to categorize data based on its sensitivity and implementing data retention policies to ensure that data is retained for the required duration and securely disposed of when no longer needed. CLI commands such as AWS S3 bucket policies or Azure Blob Storage lifecycle policies can be used to implement data classification and retention policies in cloud storage environments. Additionally, organizations must implement monitoring and auditing capabilities to track access to sensitive data and detect unauthorized access or data breaches. This involves implementing security information and event management (SIEM) systems and log management solutions to aggregate and analyze security logs and telemetry data from across the enterprise. CLI commands such as Splunk or Elasticsearch can be used to deploy SIEM solutions that provide centralized visibility into security events and anomalies. Furthermore, organizations must establish incident response and breach notification procedures to respond to security incidents in a timely manner and mitigate the impact of data breaches. This involves developing incident response plans and conducting regular incident response exercises to ensure that the organization is prepared to respond effectively to security incidents. CLI commands such as AWS Incident Response Runbooks or Azure Security Center Incident Response can be used to develop and automate incident response procedures in cloud environments. Finally, achieving regulatory compliance is an ongoing process that requires continuous monitoring and improvement. Organizations must regularly review and update their compliance measures to ensure that they remain effective in addressing evolving threats and regulatory requirements. This involves conducting regular compliance audits and assessments to identify areas for improvement and implementing corrective actions to address any deficiencies. CLI commands such as AWS Config or Azure Policy can be used to automate compliance monitoring and remediation processes in cloud environments. By following these best practices and leveraging CLI commands where applicable, organizations can achieve regulatory compliance in highly regulated industries with cloud solutions and mitigate the risk of non-compliance.

Chapter 9: Ethical Hacking and Red Teaming for Cloud Security

Performing red team exercises to test cloud security posture is a critical practice for organizations seeking to identify and mitigate potential security vulnerabilities and weaknesses. Red team exercises simulate real-world cyberattacks conducted by skilled professionals to assess an organization's defenses, detection capabilities, and response procedures. These exercises help organizations identify gaps in their security controls and processes, allowing them to strengthen their overall security posture. One of the first steps in conducting a red team exercise is to define the objectives and scope of the exercise. This involves identifying the systems, applications, and data that will be targeted during the exercise, as well as the specific tactics, techniques, and procedures (TTPs) that the red team will employ. CLI commands such as nmap, Metasploit, or SQLmap can be used to simulate various attack scenarios and assess the organization's resilience to common cyber threats. Once the objectives and scope are defined, the red team can begin the reconnaissance phase of the exercise. During this phase, the red team gathers information about the target organization's infrastructure, applications, and employees to identify potential entry points and vulnerabilities. This may involve conducting open-source intelligence (OSINT) gathering, scanning for open ports and services, and searching for publicly available information about the organization and its employees. CLI commands such as theHarvester or Recon-ng can be used to gather information about the target organization from publicly available sources such as social media, company websites, and online forums. With the reconnaissance phase complete, the red team can begin the attack phase of the exercise. During this phase, the red team attempts to exploit identified vulnerabilities and gain unauthorized access to the organization's systems, applications, and data. This may involve techniques such as phishing attacks, credential harvesting, and exploitation of known software vulnerabilities. CLI commands such as Metasploit or SQLmap can be used to launch simulated cyberattacks and attempt to compromise the organization's infrastructure and applications. As the red team conducts the attack phase, they may encounter various security controls and defenses implemented by the organization, such as firewalls, intrusion detection systems (IDS), and endpoint protection solutions. These controls are designed to detect and block malicious activity, and the red team must carefully navigate around them to achieve their objectives. CLI commands such as iptables or Windows Defender Firewall can be used to configure firewall rules and test the organization's ability to detect and respond to unauthorized access attempts. Throughout the exercise, the red team must maintain careful documentation of their actions, including the techniques used, vulnerabilities identified, and any successful compromises achieved. This documentation is essential for providing feedback to the organization and helping them understand their security strengths and weaknesses. CLI commands such as git or markdown can be used to create detailed reports documenting the red team's findings and recommendations for improving the organization's security posture. Once the attack phase is complete, the red team must conduct a thorough debriefing with the organization's security team to review the findings of the exercise and discuss potential remediation steps. This debriefing allows the organization to gain valuable insights into their security strengths and weaknesses and develop a plan for addressing any vulnerabilities identified during the exercise. CLI commands such as Zoom or Microsoft Teams can be used to conduct virtual debriefing sessions with key stakeholders and facilitate discussions about the red team's findings and recommendations. Following the debriefing, the organization should prioritize and implement remediation measures to address the vulnerabilities identified during the red team exercise. This may involve patching software vulnerabilities, updating security configurations, and enhancing employee training and awareness programs. CLI commands such as yum or apt-get can be used to install security updates and patches on Linux systems, while tools like Microsoft Endpoint Manager or WSUS can be used to deploy patches to Windows systems. Additionally, the organization should conduct regular follow-up assessments to validate the effectiveness of their remediation efforts and ensure that their security posture continues to improve over time. By regularly performing red team exercises and taking proactive steps to address security vulnerabilities, organizations can enhance their overall security posture and better protect their systems, applications, and data from cyber threats.

Implementing bug bounty programs for continuous cloud security improvement is a proactive approach adopted by organizations to identify and address security vulnerabilities in their cloud infrastructure and applications. These programs incentivize independent security researchers, also known as bug hunters or ethical hackers, to discover and report vulnerabilities in exchange for rewards. By leveraging the collective expertise of a global community of security researchers, organizations can effectively crowdsource the identification of vulnerabilities and enhance the overall security of their cloud environments. The first step in implementing a bug bounty program is to define clear guidelines and rules of engagement for participants. This includes specifying the scope of the program, outlining eligible targets for testing, and establishing criteria for submitting valid vulnerability reports. Organizations should also establish a responsible disclosure policy to ensure that vulnerabilities are reported and addressed in a timely and responsible manner. CLI commands such as git or markdown can be used to create documentation outlining the rules and guidelines for the bug bounty program. Once the guidelines are established, organizations can launch their bug bounty program on a dedicated platform or through a third-party bug bounty platform such as HackerOne, Bugcrowd, or Synack. These platforms provide a centralized platform for managing bug submissions, coordinating communication between researchers and organizations, and disbursing rewards to successful bug hunters. CLI commands such as docker-compose or kubectl can be used to deploy bug bounty platforms in containerized environments or Kubernetes clusters. As bug reports are submitted by researchers, organizations must promptly triage and validate each vulnerability to determine its severity and impact. This involves assessing the likelihood of exploitation, potential impact on the organization's systems and data, and the level of access or privileges required to exploit the vulnerability. CLI commands such as curl or wget can be used to retrieve additional information about reported vulnerabilities or test for their presence in the organization's infrastructure. Once a vulnerability is confirmed, organizations should work quickly to develop and implement appropriate remediation measures to address the issue. This may involve patching software vulnerabilities, updating configurations, or implementing additional security controls to mitigate the risk of exploitation. CLI commands such as ansible-playbook or puppet apply can be used to automate the deployment of security updates and configurations across the organization's infrastructure. Throughout the bug bounty program, organizations should maintain open communication channels with participating researchers and provide timely feedback on the status of submitted vulnerabilities. This helps build trust and collaboration between organizations and the security research community, encouraging continued participation and engagement in the bug bounty program. CLI commands such as mail or Slack can be used to communicate with researchers and provide updates on the status of their bug submissions. Additionally, organizations should regularly review and analyze the findings of the bug bounty program to identify trends, recurring issues, and areas for improvement in their cloud security posture. This includes tracking metrics such as the number of vulnerabilities identified, severity ratings, time to remediation, and overall program effectiveness. CLI commands such as grep or awk can be used to analyze and parse bug bounty reports to extract relevant metrics and insights. As the bug bounty program matures, organizations should periodically reassess and refine their program to adapt to evolving threats and technology landscapes. This may involve expanding the scope of the program, adjusting reward structures, or incorporating new testing methodologies to address emerging security challenges. CLI commands such as git or vim can be used to update documentation and guidelines for the bug bounty program as changes are implemented. By embracing bug bounty programs as part of their cloud security strategy, organizations can harness the collective intelligence of the security research community to proactively identify and address security vulnerabilities, ultimately strengthening their defenses and reducing the risk of cyberattacks.

Chapter 10: Building a Culture of Cloud Security Excellence

Cultivating security awareness training programs for cloud users is essential in fostering a culture of security consciousness within organizations transitioning to cloud environments. These programs aim to educate employees about the risks associated with cloud computing and empower them with the knowledge and skills needed to mitigate those risks. CLI commands such as ssh or scp can be used to access and transfer training materials to cloud-based learning platforms or internal repositories. One key aspect of security awareness training programs is raising awareness about common security threats and attack vectors relevant to cloud environments. This includes topics such as phishing attacks, unauthorized access, data breaches, and insecure configurations. Organizations can leverage interactive e-learning modules, simulated phishing exercises, and real-world case studies to engage employees and reinforce key security concepts. CLI commands such as wget or curl can be used to download security awareness training materials from external sources or cloud-based learning platforms. Additionally, security awareness training programs should emphasize the importance of adhering to security best practices and organizational policies when using cloud services. This includes guidelines for strong password management, secure file sharing practices, and the proper handling of sensitive data in cloud environments. CLI commands such as passwd or openssl can be used to demonstrate password management techniques or encrypt sensitive files for secure transmission. To enhance the effectiveness of security awareness training, organizations should tailor the content to the specific roles and responsibilities of different user groups within the organization. For example, IT administrators may require more in-depth training on cloud security configurations and monitoring tools, while non-technical staff may benefit from basic security hygiene tips and incident reporting procedures. CLI commands such as grep or awk can be used to filter and customize training content based on user roles and preferences. Furthermore, security awareness training programs should be delivered regularly and reinforced through ongoing communication and reinforcement activities. This includes sending out periodic security newsletters, hosting lunch-and-learn sessions, and conducting live webinars to keep employees informed about the latest security threats and best practices. CLI commands such as mail or Zoom can be used to communicate training schedules and event invitations to employees. Another important aspect of security awareness training is providing employees with practical guidance on how to recognize and respond to security incidents in cloud environments. This includes instructions on how to report suspicious emails, identify signs of unauthorized access, and escalate security concerns to the appropriate channels. CLI commands such as reportphish or ssh can be used to demonstrate incident reporting procedures or access security incident response tools. Additionally, organizations should incorporate hands-on exercises and simulations into their security awareness training programs to provide employees with practical experience in identifying and responding to security threats. This may involve conducting tabletop exercises, red team/blue team simulations, or phishing awareness drills to simulate real-world attack scenarios and test employees' response capabilities. CLI commands such as docker-compose or vagrant can be used to set up isolated training environments for hands-on exercises and simulations. To measure the effectiveness of security awareness training programs, organizations should regularly evaluate employee knowledge, attitudes, and behaviors related to cloud security. This can be done through pre- and post-training assessments, surveys, and quizzes to gauge employees' understanding of key security concepts and their adherence to security policies. CLI commands such as python or awk can be used to analyze and process survey data to identify trends and areas for improvement in security awareness training programs. Additionally, organizations should track metrics such as the number of reported security incidents, phishing click rates, and security policy compliance rates to assess the impact of security awareness training on reducing security risks in cloud environments. By cultivating security awareness training programs tailored to the needs of cloud users, organizations can empower employees to become active participants in safeguarding the organization's data and assets in the cloud. Integrating security considerations into cloud governance processes is crucial for ensuring the protection of data, applications, and infrastructure in cloud environments. One effective approach is to establish clear policies and procedures that outline security requirements and responsibilities for all stakeholders involved in cloud operations. CLI commands such as git or svn can be used to version control governance documents and policies, ensuring that they are up-to-date and accessible to relevant parties. Additionally, organizations should designate roles and responsibilities for overseeing security within the cloud governance framework. This may include appointing a dedicated cloud security team responsible for developing and enforcing security policies, conducting risk assessments, and monitoring compliance with regulatory requirements. CLI commands such as useradd or adduser can be used to create user accounts for members of the cloud security team with appropriate permissions and access levels. Another important aspect of integrating security into cloud governance processes is conducting regular risk assessments to identify potential threats and vulnerabilities in cloud environments. This involves evaluating factors such as data sensitivity, regulatory compliance requirements, and the security controls implemented by cloud service providers. CLI commands such as nmap or nessus can be used to perform vulnerability scans and penetration tests to assess the security posture of cloud infrastructure and applications. Based on the results of risk assessments, organizations can prioritize security initiatives and allocate resources effectively to address the most critical security risks. CLI commands such as grep or awk can be used to filter and analyze the output of vulnerability scans to identify high-priority vulnerabilities requiring immediate remediation. Furthermore, organizations should establish mechanisms for continuous monitoring and enforcement of security controls to ensure ongoing compliance with security policies and regulatory requirements. This may involve implementing security monitoring tools and automated compliance checks to detect and remediate security issues in real-time. CLI commands such as iptables or ufw can be used to configure firewall rules and network security groups to restrict unauthorized access to cloud resources. Additionally, organizations should implement access controls and encryption mechanisms to protect data at rest and in transit within cloud environments. This includes leveraging identity and access management (IAM) solutions to enforce least privilege principles and ensure that only authorized users have access to sensitive data and resources. CLI commands such as aws iam or gcloud iam can be used to manage IAM policies and permissions for cloud services such as AWS and Google Cloud Platform (GCP). Moreover, organizations should establish incident response procedures and protocols to effectively respond to security incidents and breaches in cloud environments. This involves defining roles and responsibilities for incident response teams, establishing communication channels for reporting and escalating security incidents, and conducting post-incident reviews to identify lessons learned and areas for improvement. CLI commands such as ssh or scp can be used to access and analyze log files and forensic data during incident response investigations. Additionally, organizations should prioritize employee training and awareness programs to educate staff about security best practices and their role in maintaining a secure cloud environment. This includes providing training on topics such as password hygiene, phishing awareness, and secure coding practices to help employees recognize and respond to security threats effectively. CLI commands such as git clone or wget can be used to download and distribute security awareness training materials to employees. In summary, integrating security considerations into cloud governance processes requires a comprehensive approach that encompasses policy development, risk management, monitoring and enforcement, incident response, and employee training. By embedding security into every aspect of cloud governance, organizations can enhance their resilience to cyber threats and ensure the confidentiality, integrity, and availability of their cloud-based assets and data.

Conclusion

In conclusion, the NIST Cloud Security book bundle offers a comprehensive journey through the intricacies of securing cloud environments, from beginner to expert level. Starting with "NIST Cloud Security 101," beginners are introduced to the fundamental concepts and principles of cloud security, laying a solid foundation for understanding the complexities ahead. As readers progress to "Navigating NIST Guidelines," intermediate users gain practical insights into implementing NIST best practices, ensuring that security measures align with industry standards and regulatory requirements.

With "Advanced Cloud Security Strategies," seasoned professionals delve deeper into NIST compliance and explore cutting-edge techniques to safeguard cloud environments against emerging cyber threats. Finally, "Mastering NIST Cloud Security" equips security professionals with the knowledge and skills needed to tackle complex challenges head-on, incorporating real-world case studies and expert insights to elevate their security posture.

Through these four books, readers gain a comprehensive understanding of NIST cloud security principles, from basic concepts to advanced strategies. By following the guidance provided in this bundle, organizations can effectively navigate the evolving landscape of cloud security, mitigating risks, and ensuring the confidentiality, integrity, and availability of their cloud-based assets. Whether you're just beginning your journey into cloud security or seeking to master advanced techniques, this book bundle serves as a valuable resource for all security professionals striving to protect their organizations in an increasingly digital world.